THE
10:10
DIET
RECIPE
BOOK

SARAH DI LORENZO
CLINICAL NUTRITIONIST

THE
10:10
DIET
RECIPE
BOOK

THE HEALTHY WAY TO LOSE 10 KILOS IN 10 WEEKS
(& keep them off forever!)

**SIMON &
SCHUSTER**

London · New York · Sydney · Toronto · New Delhi

THE 10:10 DIET RECIPE BOOK
First published in Australia in 2022 by
Simon & Schuster (Australia) Pty Limited
Suite 19A, Level 1, Building C, 450 Miller Street,
Cammeray, NSW 2062

10 9 8 7 6 5 4 3 2 1

Sydney New York London Toronto New Delhi
Visit our website at www.simonandschuster.com.au

A catalogue record for this
book is available from the
National Library of Australia

ISBN: 9781761104152

Cover and internal design: Shona Rose Design
Cover and internal photography: Andrew Young, Lantern Studio
Printed and bound in China by Asia Pacific Offset Ltd

NOTE TO READERS: The information in this book is for general purposes only. Although every
effort has been made to ensure that the contents are accurate, it must not be treated as a substitute
for qualified medical advice. Always consult a qualified medical practitioner. Neither the author nor
the publisher can be held responsible for any loss or claim arising out of the use, or misuse, of the
suggestions made or the failure to take advice.

DEDICATION

I am dedicating this book to my family members who, without knowing, played a role in my journey to get me to where I am today – for my love of nutrition, recipe creation, food appreciation and my quest to unlock the secret of how to lose weight and keep it off whilst still having it all.

To my girls and loves Charlotte, Coco and Chloe. Being your mum for me meant giving you the best possible start to life and health. Feeding you inspired me into creating recipes that were delicious, healthy, preservative-free and nutrient-dense, because I just love you all so much.

To my dad, who is a psychiatrist, I thank you for my mindset with food.

To my mum, I thank you for showing me the flaws in the weight-loss industry.

To my maternal grandparents, I thank you for teaching me about portion control and finishing a meal when I was three-quarters full.

To my paternal grandfather who was Greek and cooked amazing Mediterranean food all through my childhood, I thank you for your love of food, your culture, your love of herbs and spices, and about teaching me to eat the best produce. You were so inspiring.

Contents

FOREWORD by Sophie Falkiner

I met my gorgeous friend Sarah Di Lorenzo at a tough time in my life – I was recently separated, caring for both my beautiful young children and hustling to secure work. My cortisol was through the roof! To make matters worse, I felt terrible, because for the first time in my life, weight was sticking to me like glue and I couldn't seem to shake it no matter how hard I tried.

Through a mutual friend, I met Sarah. She was a powerhouse, part-Linda Hamilton (from *The Terminator*), part-accomplished businesswoman, part-phenomenal mother bringing up three divine daughters single-handedly. She came into my life when I needed to see other women in a similar situation to me, not being a victim of circumstance, but thriving and kicking goals.

I could immediately tell by her six-pack, no BS attitude and uncanny ability to not only find time for herself but those around her as well that this aspirational woman meant business – and there were going to be zero excuses.

Sarah truly walks the walk and talks the talk. She is not like other clinical nutritionists who might didactically tell us how to live and eat well, but don't actually do that themselves. Sarah is a living, breathing example of health, wellness and self-discipline. What I'd give to have her level of dedication and determination!

She also takes enormous pride in her work – if she takes you on as a client, she is completely and utterly committed to seeing you get results, reach your goal weight and stay there.

Sarah's approach isn't about fad dieting and starving yourself. Rather, it's about using lots of quality unprocessed ingredients in delicious and interesting ways to maintain optimum weight and health as a way of life.

When Sarah took me on as a client, we quickly forged a wonderful friendship and laughed so much as we made progress. She is one of those amazing breeds of women who likes to lift you up and empower you, as she derives so much joy in seeing and being a part of other people's successes.

Sarah also makes you accountable. I was making excuses one day to her, saying being a travel presenter on the road and eating out a lot made it hard to make healthy food choices. Quick as a flash, she gave me a cheeky smile and said, 'No problems, send me a picture of the menu and I'll tell you what to eat'. That's the extra mile Sarah will go to ensure you get results.

I'm a foodie with a ravenous penchant for all things savoury and salty – hot chips are my addiction, not to mention pasta, bread, cheese, wine, champagne and anything laden with salt and a healthy dose of fat. I've always had a big appetite, been very interested in food and even completed a nutrition certificate myself. Yet, I needed Sarah to re-educate me, especially on portions and eating to excess. Sarah is an expert in her field – she reads countless medical studies and is always up to speed on what we should be doing for our bodies to be living our best lives.

Unfortunately, it became evident my portions were humongous. Also, eating an avocado a day, telling myself it was 'healthy fats', was part of the reason the scales were not heading in the right direction! Similarly, a bit of hummus is ok, but a tub every day needs to be renegotiated. Finally, perhaps say goodbye to the accompanying culprit (the pack of rice crackers) for some carrot and celery sticks.

In my 20s and early 30s, the inside of a gym was foreign to me and I could do Wonderbra shoots in my knickers and bra after consuming a man-size plate of hot chips (with extra salt).

But in my 40s, I finally realised, with Sarah's guidance, that I wasn't going to be afforded the same metabolism and I was actually exceptionally lucky to have had it good for so long!

That had become alarmingly evident when I tried to squeeze myself into my old skinny jeans with zero success, but at least burned quite a few calories in the process!

Sarah helped me successfully navigate this time in my life by making tweaks to my quantities and the types of food I was consuming, and the best part was I wasn't starving. It was healthy weight loss done the right way. She was also realistic and allowed some alcohol in moderation, as well as my treasured cup of coffee every day. Yippee! Those pesky kilos that had crept up on me and I thought would be there forever came off like Sarah was a weight-loss magician.

In short, Sarah's programs are balanced, simple, easy, delicious and importantly, won't have you in the kitchen doing hours of laborious prep. You'll also be educated on what types of foods you should eat, how much and sometimes even at what time.

When you embark on the 10:10 Diet, you will lose weight the smart way, and it will become a way of life for you and the ones you love. I promise you'll feel more energised, your mood will be lighter and skin clearer, you'll think with more clarity, your sleep will improve and you'll have a ridiculously happy grin because you will be able to get those skinny jeans out of retirement!

Sarah is also an expert recipe creator, and this book will showcase 150 of her delectable creations that she has road tested many times to ensure they're perfect for you and your family. For breakfast (with my savoury palate), I adore the chilli scrambled eggs with Danish fetta. They're just plain yum! I also love soups, especially in the winter months, and her super creamy weight-loss soup is a crowd pleaser.

It's fantastic to make in batches for lunches on the run, too. Plus, easy one-pan meals are a godsend for the time poor, so the roasted broccoli and prawns hits all the right notes for my family, while my two teens (who both have a sweet tooth) are very partial to the chia tiramisu.

I wish Sarah every success for this book – she is one of the most hardworking, determined and inspirational women I know. Over the years, I have sent many friends and family members to see her because I know, between her amazing knowledge, down-to-earth nature and kick-arse work ethic, it's the perfect combo for getting results and, importantly, keeping them.

I highly recommend this book to anyone who wants to look and feel their best. Thank you, Sarah, for your warmth, care and beautiful friendship.

Love, Sophie xx

INTRODUCTION

About me

My passion for health, recipe creation, food, wellness and being your best self started way before I decided to be a clinical nutritionist.

I grew up in a medically oriented family. My dad is a successful psychiatrist – extremely dedicated to the health of his patients and a true doctor – and my mother was a nurse, so I always had such respect for health and medicine.

When I really think about it, it was my Greek heritage that played a very big role in my relationship with food. I grew up with my paternal grandfather living with us – he was a born and bred Greek islander from the island of Kythera and came to Australia at a young age. He brought with him the healthy eating principles of the Mediterranean diet. I grew up with his cooking, portion control, and love for and healthy relationship with food. This impacted me more than I knew. Don't get me wrong, my mum is a great cook, but my grandfather had that Mediterranean way.

My relationship with eating well also came off the back of being diagnosed with irritable bowel syndrome at the age of fifteen. While I did not have coeliac disease, I suffered from non-coeliac gluten sensitivity. This was something I was not going to accept, so I began exploring ways of treating myself. Through trial and error, I created a diet for myself that still meant I could include carbohydrates, be healthy and feel fantastic. It was while on this journey that I realised how much food really can impact quality of life. Once I worked this out, I never looked back. In hindsight, I am so relieved I did work that out at that early age as otherwise my life would have been compromised and completely different. This realisation paved the way for me to want to help others as well, hence changing my life dream of being an archaeologist to becoming a clinical nutritionist.

In my early 20s, I had spent quite a few years in the modelling industry. Interestingly, this environment further cemented my path into clinical nutrition. I saw so many females with unhealthy relationships with food that were based on staying slim. But surely there was a better way to stay slim and be healthy, too. I needed to unlock the secret of eating well, maintaining a healthy diet and feeling fabulous at the same time.

When it came to recipe creation, I would have to say that parenting really solidified this. All the recipes you will enjoy in your 10:10 Diet journey are my creations. I have always had that knack or touch when it came to cooking – just that extra sense a cook has on how things taste – and food for me needs to taste good. But when I had my first daughter and she started solids, I looked at store-bought baby foods and could not stand the thought of giving my baby something that contained preservatives, flavour enhancers and additives. So, I made everything from scratch and have done so ever since.

I believe in whole food dietary guidelines, eating food as much as possible in its true form and avoiding any additives, preservatives, artificial sweeteners or flavour enhancers.

As a single parent to three daughters, I do understand the daily juggle of kids, after-school activities, trying to find time to get in some exercise and keeping on top of the household. But one thing I really do know is that where there is a will, there is a way. It just comes down to how much you want it.

Today, I have had more than twenty years in the wellness industry. I am a fully qualified clinical nutritionist with an Advanced Diploma of Nutritional Medicine consulting from my private practice in Woollahra.

I have a completely evidence-based approach to my work, and in my spare time, I love reading the latest studies, research and findings in the nutrition field.

I have a holistic approach to health. I believe in a combination of diet, lifestyle, exercise, self-expression, social connections, self-care and always looking for self-improvement. Seeing my clients successful in their journey is what drives me, knowing they have not only reached their aesthetic goals, but have also lowered their risk of disease and increased their health span.

I am an avid exerciser and extremely proud of my three daughters, Charlotte, Coco and Chloe. I know how vital a healthy lifestyle is and that it goes hand in hand with a happy life.

I passionately believe life is short and that our best lives must be lived in the present every single day.

In the media

I am currently the resident nutritionist for Channel 7's *Weekend Sunrise* and a mainstay on Sunrise, bringing the latest health news, advice and recipes to their national audience since 2018. My recipes are always a huge success online after my segments air and the feedback is always positive after the hosts try the food.

Prior to working in television, I was resident nutritionist on a fantastic radio show, *Talking Lifestyle*, on 2UE, talking, of course, about nutritional medicine.

I am also a public speaker and really enjoy being on the speaker circuit. One of my favourite talks is 'Top 10 Strategies to Living Your Best Life'.

ABOUT THE 10:10 DIET

Background

Eating delicious healthy food, feeling vibrant and energised, and loving life is what I am passionate about, and I wanted to share my knowledge.

The 10:10 Diet was created by me to help people of all ages beyond my scope as a practitioner to achieve optimum health and vitality. I I have spent many years successfully helping people achieve healthy weight loss in clinical practice, and, through much trial, I developed the 10:10 Diet.

10:10 stands for an average weight loss of 10 kilograms in 10 weeks – the healthy way!

I do not believe in fad diets or rapid weight loss. I believe weight loss should be fat loss. I believe in a healthy body image and realistic healthy goal weight. A healthy weight for your height. I believe in taking care of our health along the way, always correcting any nutritional deficiencies and lowering the risk of disease.

When I started creating the 10:10 Diet, I carefully crafted it to be a healthy diet that put the body into a ketogenic stage – a fat loss diet while still being healthy. I have only ever believed that weight loss should be fat loss. When people rapidly lose weight, they lose fat, fluid and muscle. I see this as dangerous to the body as long-term yoyo dieting leads to muscle loss and advanced aging. I want to preserve muscle and keep the body wonderfully hydrated, so the 10:10 Diet was created.

For the better part of 30 years, I have been the same weight, outside of having three babies. While I spent much of my time working out how to feel great, enjoy life and food guilt-free, and still be at a healthy weight, the weight-loss industry was always coming up with something new.

When I was in my early 20s, the obsession was with low fat – there were new highly processed products popping up on the market that promised to lower cholesterol and help with weight loss. Buzz words back then were 'fat-free', 'zero', 'lite', 'sugar-free' and 'low-fat'. These words for many back then meant health – when in fact they did the opposite, and this is evident in the growing obesity statistics.

With the fear of fat and the belief that fat makes you fat, people ate a lot more refined carbohydrates, and this is linked to diseases such as type 2 diabetes, cardiovascular disease and obesity. Witnessing this throughout my life further drove me to teach people the true and healthy way to lose weight and keep it off.

All of this has been taken into consideration in creating the 10:10 Diet.

Aims

The goal of the 10:10 Diet is to teach you long-term health and wellness. Not only do you learn how to eat well, lose weight, sleep better, and have more energy, but you will also learn new recipes and food preparation, and understand the importance of not skipping meals, all while increasing your health span.

You will enjoy so many new recipes to include in your 10:10 Diet journey. All recipes have been created by me to make sure you are getting nutrient-rich food that will also keep you full between meals and still taste absolutely delicious. In fact, something I hear a lot from people is just how much they love the recipes, and how fantastic it is to lose weight and still love food.

What is the 10:10 Diet?

The 10:10 Diet is a 10-week healthy weight-loss program that encompasses three main methods, all carefully put together to make your journey a success. It's also designed to teach you a new style of eating so you can feel positive about yourself, be energised, have a youthful glow and feel in control. It is a program that teaches a healthy lifestyle. This is not a fad diet or in any way designed to be rapid weight loss – it is healthy weight loss.

The foundation of this program is about living your best life, and by that, I mean healthy weight, vitality, positivity, energy and glow. I have lived this way all my life and want to share my secrets for success with you.

As a clinical nutritionist, I have made sure the menu is nutrient dense, nutritionally balanced for weight loss, and healthy.

The three main concepts of the 10:10 Diet are:

1. Healthy, low-carbohydrate, high-protein meals.
2. 600-calorie days – the key to accelerating weight loss.
3. Healthy detox – a time to focus on yourself.

Program guidelines

The 10:10 Diet is designed in phases. These have been carefully put together to take care of your health along the way. The initial stages of the program are set out to get you into the swing of it.

The program runs week to week so pick your start day. Many people start on a Monday, but this is entirely up to you. When it comes to starting the program, my advice is don't procrastinate; there is never a good time to start as birthdays, events, Easter, Christmas and other festivities will always come about. Just switch up your mindset and start now.

Each week of the 10-week program has a new focus:

*   Week 1: Education, preparation and getting into ketosis
*   Week 2: Learning the first 600-calorie day
*   Week 3: Getting into the swing of it
*   Week 4: Establishing good habits
*   Week 5: Detox introduction
*   Week 6: Detoxing the healthy way and making time for you
*   Week 7: Double the 600-calorie days
*   Week 8: Cementing your new lifestyle
*   Week 9: Celebrating accelerated weight loss
*   Week 10: Success and the way forward – your 'new normal'.

The first week is really about getting prepared. It is a big change for many people and a completely new style of eating. The body is slowly being depleted of glucose and glycogen, putting the body into a healthy state of ketosis or fat burning. It is for this reason that I wanted the first week to be a healthy meal plan so there is a good flow of energy throughout the day while this metabolic fuel source is changing.

Week 2 is the introduction of the 600-calorie days. I have carefully positioned the first 600-calorie day on Day 11 of the program. This is so I can be sure the body is in ketosis at this stage. Tell-tale signs of ketosis are a difference in smell of urine and taste in breath, lowered appetite and clarity of mind. I also love these 600-calorie days because there are so many benefits of reduced calorie intake, such as:

*   losing weight
*   lowering your risk of disease
*   lowering blood pressure
*   lowering inflammation
*   increasing life and health span
*   improving energy levels
*   boosting your mood
*   improving blood sugar levels
*   boosting brain health
*   helping anti-aging.

The 600-calorie days in the program are designed for two reasons. First, to accelerate weight loss and secondly, as a great tool for when you are at your goal weight and in maintenance mode. They are designed for you to have 600 calories during the course of the day. The menu in the food plan sits at approximately 500 calories on some days and this is because I want to make allowances for you to enjoy milk with a coffee or tea. Yes, we can't forget liquid calories, and let's face it – a low-calorie day without your coffee or tea would be really challenging.

Some tips to help you get through your 600-calorie day are:

- keep busy
- drink lots of water
- go to bed early
- enjoy herbal tea
- remember your goals.

Weeks 2, 3 and 4 include just one 600-calorie day.

Weeks 5 and 6 are a two-week mini detox. I put this in the program at this stage to change the pace, but also as a time to reflect. I see the detoxing weeks as a gift to yourself rather than a time to feel deprived. I have found throughout my years as a practitioner that a weight-loss plateau can come around the four-week mark. There are many reasons for a plateau but the detox can help bypass this.

I do allow coffee and tea but not alcohol during these weeks. The menu is very specific to detoxing guidelines. I also encourage you in these weeks to remember your goals and do something you love, such as attending a dance class, visiting a gallery or having a massage. Be kind to yourself. Set more goals, do a spring clean and get ready for the last phase of the program.

Weeks 7, 8, 9 and 10 are all designed for accelerated weight loss. You are well into the program, you have reset with the detox, you know how to get through your 600-calorie days, and you have learnt how to food prep well. There are many recipes you now have down pat and your fitness regime is well and truly established. These last weeks, when done with compliance, will amp up the weight loss considerably, getting you ready for the maintenance phase.

Benefits of the 10:10 Diet

When you make that decision to start on the 10:10 Diet journey, your initial motivation is really to lose weight. But there are so many amazing benefits of the 10:10 Dict way of life that you will experience. I love reading all the non-scale victories people have and just hearing about how their lives have changed.

The obvious benefit is that you will lose weight – this is a given. But some general benefits of the 10:10 Diet are learning about:

- portion sizes
- detoxing the right way
- healthy snacking
- the value of 600-calorie days
- the importance of exercise
- integrating nutritious eating into your lifestyle
- long-term weight maintenance
- adequate hydration
- the ways that weight loss can be delicious and easy
- a new way of life.

The benefits continue and it is these health victories I absolutely love! Honestly, it just makes me so happy when I see the changes in people. Knowing that my unique program has changed the course of their health and aging is an incredible reward as a practitioner.

It is a good idea to get blood tests done before you start on the program and then get them done again after. You will be astounded by just how much your health status has improved. I always recommend asking the doctor for a full blood count (FBC), liver function, lipid profile, iron studies, C-reactive protein (CRP), vitamin D and thyroid.

When you start to eat real food; remove all processed foods, soft drinks and junk from your diet; and include the 10:10 Diet guidelines, the gift of long-term health and wellness is something you are giving yourself without even realising. It is a magnificent by-product!

Health victories of the 10:10 Diet are:

1. **Weight loss is fat loss.** The 10:10 Diet is designed to reduce body fat, not muscle and fluid. This is so important and the healthy way to lose weight. Fat is inflammatory to the body and should not be seen as a reservoir of energy, but rather as a disease state.

2. **Lowering your risk of disease.** When you lose fat, you lower your risk of diseases such as type 2 diabetes, cardiovascular disease, hypertension, depression, obesity and metabolic syndrome, to name a few.

3. **Reducing inflammation.** A change to a healthy diet will lower your inflammation, which in turn lowers your risk of diseases, including some cancers.

4. **Metabolic management.** The 10:10 Diet will help manage your metabolism, by improving your blood sugar, potentially reversing diabetes, lowering blood pressure, lowering cholesterol, reducing the risk of dementia and reducing the risk of stroke.

5. **Extending your health span.** We are all living longer than ever before, but this does not mean increasing health span. By getting to a healthy weight with nutrient-dense food, good sleep, regular exercise and minimal alcohol, you are increasing your health span and therefore quality of life.

There are also many more non-scale health victories that can be more rewarding than the number on the scale. These include:

- a better relationship with food
- better skin
- better sleep
- more energy
- improved fitness level
- no more bloating
- regular exercise
- losing inches (your weight might remain the same)
- better digestion
- managing stress, emotions and boredom eating
- no more sweet tooth
- a reduction in pharmaceutical medications
- fewer migraines or headaches
- better focus and clearer thinking
- a reduction in alcohol
- learning a new style of cooking
- most importantly, feeling confident and loving life!

As you can see, the 10:10 Diet is so much more than a weight-loss program. Research shows that to change a way of life you need to participate in a new way of doing things for an average of 66 days. Then, the chances of you sticking with this as the foundation of your normal is a very real possibility.

Now you have a much broader range of nutrient-rich recipes to choose. I'm sure many will become family favourites.

General guidelines for the 10:10 Diet

Coffee is fine to enjoy. If adding milk, I suggest you change to almond milk as it has the lowest calorie count. Avoid adding sugar and sweeteners to hot beverages. Black coffee is best for weight loss as it does get rid of hunger pangs and studies have shown it can increase metabolism. Just be mindful of your milk.

Alcohol is fine in moderation. I am a realist and know that if I told people to avoid alcohol for 10 weeks compliance could be poor. The only time I suggest you avoid alcohol is during the two-week detox. If you truly want to shift weight, alcohol avoidance is the way to go, but if you would prefer to drink then my guidelines are:

- five nights a week alcohol-free
- two nights a week alcohol
- no more than 7 units per week (a unit is 150ml wine or 25ml spirits)
- avoid mixers, such as soft drinks
- avoid beer.

Exercise is a prerequisite for my program. Did you know that we lose fat through our breath? That explains why cardiovascular exercise is fantastic for weight loss. My exercise guidelines are simple – 45 minutes of cardiovascular exercise four times a week, such as power walking, running, jogging, swimming or cycling. For those of you who don't like those options, try a dance class. If you have not exercised in a long time, just start with power walking and build on it.

Water intake is like a prescription. I know it sounds counterintuitive but drinking water really does help with weight loss. It supports our liver, where we metabolise our fats and where the creation of ketones takes place. It reduces water weight in the body as well. Adequate hydration is 30 ml per kilogram of body weight per day. For example, if you weigh 60 kilograms, you should drink 1.8 litres of water a day.

Make sure you are getting enough water – you can include herbal teas and mineral water in your water count. You may need to set reminders in the beginning, but before you know it, it will become a habit and you will start to crave it.

Sleep is king! I always say this. Lack of sleep will contribute to weight gain. Compliance with a weight-loss program is much harder when you are dealing with fatigue. Make sure you are getting my recommendation of seven to eight hours of sleep a night. This may be a struggle for some, but my tips to help you get a better night's sleep are:

- exercise every day
- avoid alcohol
- make sure the room is conducive to good sleep
- take some magnesium before bed (about 300 mg)
- don't eat too late – aim to have dinner around 6 pm
- have a relaxing bath in Epsom salts
- remove technology from the bedroom
- practise meditation.

If you are prone to stress, boredom and emotional eating, you need to get on top of this for long-term success with weight-loss maintenance. When these behaviours present themselves, stop, reflect and be kind to yourself. If you are stressed, talk to someone or go for a big walk. If you are emotional, then go and treat yourself to a manicure or have a rest and, if you are bored, find something to do. Food is NOT the solution and will only make you feel worse.

The 10:10 Diet and its accompanying lifestyle is the foundation for you to build upon when you embark on weight-loss maintenance. Once you have established the 10:10 Diet principles into your life you will never look back. What you put into the program is what you will get out of it. People who are committed and dedicated will get incredible results – I have seen this time and time again.

Your 10:10 Diet tool kit to get started

Welcome to getting started on your journey. I always say the key to success is preparation, and this includes getting your 10:10 Diet tool kit ready. There are different aspects to getting started on this journey to guarantee you comprehensive success. Have a chat to loved ones, family members or housemates and tell them what you are doing so they can be encouraging and supportive.

Join my private Facebook group, The Sarah Di Lorenzo Community, where you will meet amazing likeminded people who all share the same goals as you. Inspire and support each other. It is such a fantastic community full of kind people who, like you, are on a journey to live their best life.

Importantly, it is about you as an individual and what your start point looks like. I am a big believer in keeping track of your progress – this will keep you inspired to keep going. You can write in a special journal or notebook, or use your computer or phone. Plus, it is something you can always look back on years later to remember what you did. While the menu is set out for you, you may chop and change the recipes, keep track of your food with your journal, sit down at the end of the day with a cup of peppermint tea and spend five minutes on yourself tracking your food. I love to set goals and when you achieve them it is a great feeling.

Set some time aside the day before you start the program and write down your goals, outlining what you want to achieve. These can include both scale and non-scale victories.

As you are starting the program, I recommend that you:

- Take all your measurements. Women, measure your hips, thighs, bust, waist and upper arms. Men, measure around the abdomen. Write your measurements down with the date.
- Weigh yourself upon waking. When you do weigh yourself, do it at the same time of day. I don't think daily weighing is a good idea as it can have adverse reactions. Every few days jump on the scale and see how you are going.
- Take a photo of yourself in your underwear or swimwear, just to see where you have come from. It is worth it.
- When your clothing starts getting too baggy, get rid of it or donate it to charity. You are never going to fit back into these clothes again and keeping them is not the right mindset – there is no 'just in case'. That was the old you. If you have clothing you love that is too big, take it to the tailor to resize it when you are at your goal weight.

Some appliances that are fantastic to have are a bullet blender and a spiralizer. If you don't have a spiralizer then a potato peeler will work just as well. The bullet blender is really important for all the delicious smoothies and protein shakes you will find in this recipe book. If you have a handheld blender, it will work as well.

FREQUENTLY ASKED QUESTIONS

Over the years of people successfully doing the 10:10 Diet, a series of frequently asked questions have emerged. The questions arise as there are many different types of people who do the program and have different levels of exercise, coffee consumption, sleep, dietary requirements, taste buds and compliance, to name a few things.

Q: Can I switch proteins in recipes?

A: Absolutely. Anything from the recommended protein list is fine. That is, fish, chicken, cheese, eggs, lamb, beef, tofu, tempeh, kangaroo, turkey, pork, veal, duck, prawns, octopus, scallops, mussels and oysters. However, no processed meat or bacon should be eaten.

Q: Can I repeat meals?

A: Yes, of course. All meals are carefully balanced to make sure you get the right macronutrients for the program. This may help many with food preparation as well.

Q: Can I exercise on the 600-calorie days?

A: Yes. This is an individual choice, though. Many people find they are hungrier on exercise days, so compliance could be poor. Again, it's trial and error. I personally do it without any problem.

Q: What if I don't like apple cider vinegar?

A: That's fine, leave it out and replace it with lemon water. To make lemon water, squeeze 1 lemon into 250 ml warm water. Add ½ teaspoon raw honey if you would like it sweetened. These drinks aid detox and help lower blood sugar, help with weight loss, are important for healthy skin and support digestion.

Q: What if I don't like lemon water?

A: Try water with fresh cucumber or mint, or replace with green tea.

Q: Can I have a cheat day?

A: I don't agree with the mindset of a 'cheat day'. I do understand there may be days that are harder than others. When at your goal weight, you can have days where you enjoy more foods as well as some types of dessert. A weekly cheat day will only stall the weight-loss journey and pull you out of ketosis. It's just not worth it and falls into the category of reward eating, which is not healthy.

Q: What if I am going to a wedding or party that has a sit-down dinner?

A: Go ahead and enjoy it. Do a 600-calorie day the next day. Life is too short not to have fun.

Q: How do you navigate a buffet?

A: Just serve yourself as you would at home with a palm-sized portion of protein and 1.5 cups of salad or vegetables. Don't go back for seconds.

Q: Is there an easy way to do the 10:10 Diet and still feed the family?

A: Yes, definitely. Make the 10:10 Diet meal and then do a side of carbohydrate for the family, such as mashed potatoes, rice, baked potatoes, pasta or bread. Otherwise, do what I call three-part meals: part 1 protein, part 2 vegetables and part 3 carbohydrate.

Q: What is the guideline for dressing?

A: One teaspoon per meal. Make your own dressings with olive oil, lemon juice, garlic, salt and pepper.

Q: How do you get through hunger on fast days?

A: Drink lots of water. Keep busy. Drink black coffee (but only in the morning). Go to bed early. If desperate, have some celery (two stalks) or one cucumber.

Q: Why does my weight loss slow down after the third week?

A: Generally, in the first two weeks, we lose water weight as well as fat. The water weight is gone by the second week. Then the weight loss is fat loss. This is the right way to lose weight.

Q: Do I need to do the detox?

A: This is up to you. If you want to skip Weeks 5 and 6, that is fine. Just repeat Weeks 9 and 10. The detox is designed to change the pace of the program, a time to stop and reflect, goal set and be ready for the last four weeks.

Q: Can I drink coffee in the detox?

A: Yes, this is completely fine. Just try to drink one per day. I would rather that then not doing the detox at all.

Q: What do I do if I have broken the diet?

A: Get straight back on that day or the next morning. Never delay it. We are all human and life can get in the way for many. The most important thing is that you get back on track rather than pack it in and revert to ways you weren't happy with.

Q: What protein powder is best?

A: This is personal choice – some like a pea protein powder, some like whey protein powder. So long as the protein powder is around 20 grams per serve, low in sugar and carbs, then it is fine.

Q: What are the best swaps for tofu?

A: Chicken and fish would be the best swap.

Q: Can I drink kombucha or flavoured mineral water?

A: Make sure the kombucha is low in sugar and good quality. Mineral water is fine, but I do not recommend flavoured mineral water.

Q: How much coffee and tea can I drink?

A: If it's black, then around 3–6 cups a day is fine. If you add milk and sugar, then that's a different story. Without knowing it you can add hundreds of calories into your day and wonder why you are not losing weight.

Q: What if I don't like some of the vegetables in the recipes?

A: You can add whatever vegetables you like to the recipes, but just not potato or sweet potato.

Q: Can I repeat the program if I have more than 10 kilograms to lose?

A: Yes, absolutely. I have had people do the program three times in a row as they have had to lose 30 kilograms or more.

Q: Can I do the program if I have food intolerances?

A: Yes, you can. If you have a dairy intolerance, substitute with soy or almond products and use coconut yoghurt. For egg allergies, choose another meal from the program that works for you. For any other intolerances, have more from the program of what you can eat.

Q: What can I do if I don't get time to food prep?

A: There is always a solution. Keep a protein bar and a small bag of nuts in your bag or in the car. For meals, you can always quickly prepare protein and salad, just keep to the palm-sized portion of protein and 1.5 cups of salad or vegetables. Restaurants and cafes are always accommodating, as well as food halls. Short of that, head to the supermarket and grab a salad bag and a tin of tuna and you are in business.

I really hope I have covered all your questions. Keep going on your 10:10 Diet journey to health and wellness – it is worth it.

ABOUT THE RECIPES

In this book, I have created a lot more snacks to cover all different taste buds and keep it interesting for you. As for my smoothie recipes, they are so popular I have added in a good variety for you to change things up along the way.

I have carefully considered the vegans and vegetarians who have embraced the 10:10 Diet, and you will find that there is a great variety of recipes to choose from. I know I love vegetarian and vegan meals even though I am not one. But don't forget, if there are other recipes you like, you can always change the protein to something of your choice – just make the swap.

Soups and stews are so popular in the cooler months, and I have had many people write to me over the years about finding the right soup to still enjoy but help with weight loss. I am so excited to share my favourite soup recipes with you that have been carefully constructed with my unique weight-loss soup formula.

As for the 600-calorie day recipes, these days play a very important role in the 10:10 Diet formula. They are designed to keep the weight loss going and add another dimension to the program. They are a great solution to do the next day if you've overindulged, which is a part of life, by the way. I am sharing so many more incredibly delicious low-calorie recipes that have been carefully calorie counted with the goal of still being delicious. Nothing is worse than a tasteless low-calorie day!

I have also considered the breakfast lovers in this book. I always insist on starting your day with a meal – big or small. I am a firm believer in getting the digestion going and providing the body with energy for the morning. In fact, research shows that people who are breakfast eaters take in fewer calories than those who skip breakfast. You will find some sweet breakfast options as well as savoury.

Lunch is probably my favourite meal of the day. No matter what, I will always enjoy a good lunch. I have shared a good variety of my favourite lunches for healthy weight loss. These recipes can also be interchanged for dinner.

In my dinner menu, I have also made sure I have covered a good range. You have dinners to enjoy in any season. Just like lunch, if you want to interchange these you can.

Halfway through your 10:10 Diet journey is the two-week detox. I look at these two weeks as way more than a detox. When people think of detox, they think of something negative. I see it as the opposite – a time to stop, reflect, avoid alcohol, goal set and eat a certain way. I have included recipes that are designed to complement detoxing but are also rich in flavour.

I could not forget those with a sweet tooth – I have one, too. But what about a guilt-free sweet tooth? I have included some of my absolute favourite guilt-free dessert recipes. You will notice that when I do put them in my menu plan, I will remove the mid-afternoon snack. As with the 600-calorie days after an overindulgence, the skipping of an afternoon snack will balance out the dessert.

I hope you enjoy these recipes as much as I do. Knowing you are losing body fat with nutrient-rich delicious food and feeling full is my goal. Once you hit your goal weight, these recipes can be part of the formula for keeping weight off for life, lowering your risk of disease, being in control of your health and having the confidence to live your best life in health and wellness.

I wish you all the best on this journey, and I hope you enjoy all my delicious recipes along the way, all designed to satiate, inspire and nourish you.

Protein bars, smoothies and shakes

Throughout the menu, you will find I have put in some protein bars, smoothies and shakes. These are optional, and if you choose to not include them, it doesn't affect the outcome. There are lots of snacks you can interchange and many delicious breakfast options.

But there are also many people who really like the convenience of grabbing a protein bar or doing a shake in the morning. One of the benefits of including these is that you always have a plan B. You can throw a protein bar in your bag if you are in a rush or keep them in your drawer at work. In the morning, you can very easily make up a shake or smoothie and away you go. I love smoothies and have been making them for my family for years, especially for my daughters. It is such a great way to make a meal so nutrient dense.

In the smoothies and protein shakes there is protein powder. I love a good-quality protein powder and it does play a very important role in keeping you full between meals.

Here are my guidelines for protein powder and protein bars:

Guidelines for a protein bar (60 grams)
200 calories
20 grams protein
3 grams carbohydrates
2.4 grams sugars
6 grams fat

**Guidelines for protein powder
(per serve of 20 grams)**
100 calories
18 grams protein
1.5 grams carbohydrates
1 gram fat

For those of you with lactose intolerance, consider many of the non-whey options available made from pea protein or soy that you may tolerate well.

So now you have your tool kit packed and ready to go, it is time to go shopping!

Recipes

Welcome to enjoying lots more recipes that you can incorporate into the 10-week program and interchange as you please. Many people have their favourite recipes, but I am going to share many more of my wonderful creations for you to enjoy.

The basic formula for all my recipes is based on portions and control.
A guide per meal is:

- for protein, cover your palm
- for fat, cover your thumb
- for carbohydrates, use a cupped hand (one for women, two for men)
- for vegetables, use three closed fists
- for fruit, use one closed fist.

When you are in maintenance mode, this guide will be something we use to build on, remembering that when you are doing weight loss, your body is in deficit, hence the weight loss. So, it only makes sense to use this as the scaffolding to build on when at goal weight.

All my recipes are my creations and made from my heart with love. I believe foods should taste delicious, and you should never feel deprived or like you are on a diet when doing my program.

BREAKFAST

BREAKFAST OPTIONS

TO KEEP YOUR 10:10 DIET JOURNEY ALWAYS DELISH

It is often stated that breakfast is the most important meal of the day and I always recommend you don't skip it. When we start our day with a great breakfast, it stimulates digestion and metabolism. Research shows we process much more of what we eat in the morning than later in the day.

I have found over the years that many people skip breakfast and can easily go through to lunch on only coffee, and this is one of the first things I correct when I start nutritional programs with them.

My unique formula for breakfast is to always make sure there is some kind of protein involved to keep you satiated throughout the morning with that slow release of energy, so you are not hunting around for food not long after.

It is always good to change things up with our meals and get a broad spectrum of vitamins and minerals in the diet, plus the diversity of foods is excellent for gut health.

Here are some of my favourite breakfast recipes.

Cottage cheese, banana and almond butter

SERVES 1

Ingredients

3 tablespoons cottage cheese

1 frozen banana, sliced

1 tablespoon almond butter

2 tablespoons milk (almond is my recommendation)

1 teaspoon chia seeds

Method

1. In a food processor, blend the cottage cheese, banana, almond butter and milk until smooth. Place in a bowl.

2. Sprinkle with chia seeds.

HEALTH FACT

Cottage cheese is an excellent source of protein and is low in calories. Half a cup of low-fat cottage cheese has only 80 calories. Because of its high protein content, it is great for building muscle mass and is a popular food among athletes. It is also rich in B vitamins that are excellent for energy, as well as calcium for bone health and selenium that supports thyroid health.

Sarah's baked mushroom with egg

SERVES 1

Ingredients (per mushroom)

1 large field mushroom

olive oil

salt and pepper

1 egg

2 teaspoons grated parmesan cheese

1 tablespoon chopped parsley and chives, to garnish

Method

1. Preheat oven to 200°C. Wipe the mushroom clean with a damp paper towel. Remove the stem and gills.

2. Brush the mushroom with olive oil on both sides. Sprinkle with salt and pepper. Place on a lined baking tray in the middle of the oven with the grill on. Grill both sides for a few minutes, until golden brown.

3. Remove the mushroom from the oven. Drain any liquids.

4. Break the egg into the mushroom and sprinkle with cheese. Bake for 15 minutes, until the egg white is cooked.

5. To serve, sprinkle with salt and pepper and garnish with parsley and chives. Delicious!

 HEALTH FACT

Mushrooms are a fabulous source of fibre, protein and antioxidants, and are low in calories. They are also an excellent source of selenium, which is great for thyroid health. Research shows they may also lower the risk of health conditions, such as heart disease and Alzheimer's.

Sarah's blueberry chia jam and yoghurt

MAKES 1 JAR OF JAM TO KEEP

Ingredients

2 cups blueberries

2 tablespoons chia seeds

1 tablespoon raw honey

Breakfast

2 tablespoons good-quality Greek yoghurt

2 tablespoons blueberry chia jam

Method

1. Add the blueberries to a saucepan and cook over low heat for about 5 minutes until they reduce and are soft then mash with a potato masher or fork.

2. Add the chia seeds and honey; stir to combine and cook for a further 3 minutes.

3. Pour into a sterilised jar. The chia seeds will continue to soften and expand. When cool, refrigerate and keep up to 2 weeks.

HEALTH FACT

Chia seeds contain quercetin, which is an antioxidant that can lower blood pressure and reduce your risk of developing heart disease. Chia is also an excellent source of calcium, which is great for building and maintaining strong bones.

Cottage cheese, apple and cinnamon

SERVES 1

Ingredients

2 tablespoons cottage cheese

½ apple, chopped

½ teaspoon cinnamon

Method

Spoon the cottage cheese into a bowl, top with chopped apple and sprinkle with cinnamon.

 HEALTH FACT

Cinnamon is a great source of antioxidants and also has anti-inflammatory properties. It may also help lower blood sugar and fight diabetes. Cinnamon increases insulin sensitivity by making insulin more effective at moving glucose to the cells.

Boiled eggs and zucchini

SERVES 1

Ingredients

2 eggs

1 zucchini

Method

1. To soft boil the eggs, drop them into boiling water for 4 minutes.

2. Chop the zucchini into finger-sized pieces and then steam. An easy way to do this is to steam the zucchini over the boiling water of the eggs.

3. Serve in egg cups, with salt and pepper. Enjoy by dipping the zucchini into the runny egg yolk.

 HEALTH FACT

Eggs are one of the healthiest foods you can eat. They are rich in vitamins, minerals, protein and omega-3 fatty acids. A large egg has around 75 calories so is a fantastic choice for healthy weight loss. My guidelines with eggs are no more than two per day.

Scrambled eggs and kimchi

SERVES 1

Ingredients

2 eggs

½ teaspoon olive oil

1 tablespoon kimchi

parsley, to garnish

salt and pepper

Method

1. Whisk the 2 eggs until combined. Add the olive oil to a frying pan over medium low heat then pour in the egg mixture.

2. Add the kimchi and scramble the eggs.

3. To serve, garnish with parsley and season with salt and pepper.

HEALTH FACT

Kimchi is a staple food in Korea and is made with salted fermented vegetables. It is low in calories but is loaded with iron, folate, vitamin K, vitamin B6 and antioxidants, making it a great addition to your diet. As it is fermented, kimchi is rich in probiotics, making it excellent for gut health. Probiotics have also been shown to improve heart health by lowering cholesterol and inflammation.

Strawberry mint chia breakfast bowl

SERVES 1

Ingredients

2 tablespoons chia

100 ml water

50 ml almond milk

½ teaspoon cinnamon

½ teaspoon vanilla extract

5 strawberries

1 tablespoon chopped fresh mint leaves

Method

1. Soak the chia, water, almond milk, cinnamon and vanilla in a bowl overnight.

2. In the morning, stir the chia mixture well and chop the strawberries.

3. Serve the chia topped with strawberries and garnished with mint leaves.

HEALTH FACT

Strawberries are an excellent choice for weight loss as they are low in calories with just 49 calories per cup. They are also an excellent source of vitamin C, which is important for immunity. Just one serving – or about eight strawberries – provides more vitamin C than an orange.

Poached eggs and spring onions

SERVES 1

Ingredients

2 eggs

½ teaspoon olive oil

2 spring onions, sliced

salt and pepper

Method

1. Poach the eggs.

2. In a frying pan, add the oil and spring onions and cook over medium heat until brown and caramelised, about 2 minutes.

3. Transfer to a plate. Top the spring onions with the poached eggs and season with salt and pepper.

 HEALTH FACT

Spring onions have anti-bacterial and anti-inflammatory properties and can help fight against colds and flu. They are rich in fibre and are excellent for gut health. Spring onions also contain calcium, vitamin C, vitamin A and vitamin B6, making them an excellent addition to meals. They are low in calories and can be cooked or eaten raw.

Breakfast salad

SERVES 1

Ingredients

1 egg

1 cup chopped iceberg lettuce

¼ avocado, sliced

¼ cup chopped fresh basil
    and coriander

salt and pepper

1 teaspoon olive oil

1 lemon, juiced

Method

1. Drop the egg in boiling water for 8 minutes. Remove and cool under cold water.

2. Combine lettuce, avocado and herbs in a bowl. Slice the egg over the top. Season with salt and pepper and drizzle with olive oil and lemon juice.

 Avocados are an excellent addition to any meal. They are rich in fibre and omega-3 fatty acids and are great for heart health and keeping you full. Coriander is known to help support the liver, which is detoxifying the body all the time. Coriander is also great for gut health, heart health and is rich in antioxidants.

Baked egg

SERVES 1

Ingredients

½ cup chopped spinach

½ teaspoon olive oil

1 egg

1 tomato, sliced

salt and pepper

Method

1. Preheat oven to 180°C. Using a ramekin baking dish, add chopped spinach, olive oil and then tomato.

2. Crack the egg over the top and place in the oven for 15 minutes. Season to taste and serve.

 HEALTH FACT

Spinach is an excellent choice for healthy weight loss as it is low in calories, rich in vitamin C, vitamin A, folic acid and calcium, and is high in insoluble fibre, making it great for digestion.

Yoghurt, seeds and fruit

SERVES 1

Ingredients

½ cup Greek yoghurt

½ teaspoon vanilla extract

½ teaspoon ground ginger

¼ teaspoon ground cinnamon

1 tablespoon chia seeds

1 tablespoon pumpkin seeds

¼ cup berries or chopped fruit of your choice

½ teaspoon maple syrup

mint leaves, to garnish

Method

1. In a bowl, add the yoghurt, vanilla, ground ginger and ground cinnamon and mix well.

2. Add the seeds, berries or fruit and maple syrup and garnish with mint. Delicious!

 HEALTH FACT *Greek yoghurt is protein-rich so will help you feel full for longer. It also contains probiotics so is great for gut health. Greek yoghurt can also improve bone health as it is rich in calcium and may help to lower blood pressure and reduce the risk of type 2 diabetes.*

Frozen yoghurt and berry bake

SERVES 4

Ingredients

2 cups Greek yoghurt

1 tablespoon honey

1 teaspoon vanilla extract

1 cup chopped strawberries

¼ cup desiccated coconut

Method

1. In a bowl, mix the yoghurt with the honey and vanilla until well combined.

2. Line a baking tray then pour the yoghurt mixture on top.

3. Add the chopped strawberries evenly over the top of the yoghurt. Sprinkle the coconut over the top and then freeze for at least 6 hours.

4. Once frozen, break the mix into smaller pieces. Serving size is ¼ of the tray. Enjoy on a summer morning. Easy!

HEALTH FACT

Coconut contains fibre and fat in the form of medium-chain triglycerides (MCTs). Your body metabolises MCTs differently from other types of fats. They are absorbed directly from your small intestine and rapidly used for energy. These types of fats may benefit weight loss, digestion, brain health and immunity and can also help regulate blood glucose levels.

Sweet and green protein shake

SERVES 1

Ingredients

1 scoop (20 g) protein powder

4 ice cubes

150 ml water

1 cup chopped spinach

1 kiwi fruit

Method

Blitz all ingredients in a bullet blender or use a handheld blender and enjoy.

Kiwi fruit are rich in vitamin C. Just one kiwi fruit gives you 66 per cent of your daily recommended requirement of vitamin C. Vitamin C boosts the immune system to help ward off disease, increases iron absorption and is essential for the synthesis of collagen.

Protein shake with antioxidants

SERVES 1

Ingredients

1 scoop (20 g) protein powder

4 ice cubes

150 ml water

½ cup blueberries

Method

Blitz all ingredients in a bullet blender or use a handheld blender and enjoy.

HEALTH FACT

Blueberries are so rich in antioxidants they could be hailed king of antioxidant-rich foods. We need antioxidants to fight free radicals. Free radicals damage healthy cells in our body by stealing electrons from them. Blueberries are also high in fibre and low in carbohydrates, making them excellent for healthy weight loss. Other health benefits of blueberries include lowering blood pressure and improving heart health.

Baked apple

SERVES 1

Ingredients

1 apple

2 tablespoons oats

½ teaspoon ground cinnamon

2 teaspoons maple syrup

1 teaspoon vanilla extract

1 tablespoon Greek yoghurt

1 teaspoon crushed roasted almonds

Method

1. Preheat oven to 180°C. Cut off the top of the apple and scoop out the core and some flesh so it resembles a bowl.

2. In another bowl, mix the oats, cinnamon, maple syrup and vanilla. Add the mix to the apple and place in the oven in a baking dish for 25 minutes.

3. Once ready, serve topped with yoghurt and sprinkled with almonds.

HEALTH FACT

Oats are an excellent choice for helping to lower cholesterol. They are rich in complex carbohydrates and fibre. Oats contain powerful antioxidants that can reduce blood pressure, promote healthy gut bacteria and help keep you feeling full.

Ricotta pots

SERVES 1

Ingredients

3 tablespoons ricotta

½ teaspoon ground cinnamon

½ teaspoon ground ginger

½ teaspoon vanilla extract

¼ cup blueberries

½ teaspoon maple syrup

Method

1. Add the ricotta, cinnamon, ginger and vanilla extract to a bowl and mix well. Transfer to a little pot, cup or small bowl.

2. Add the berries and maple syrup and serve.

HEALTH FACT

Ricotta is a healthier choice when it comes to cheeses. It has less fat and salt than other cheeses but is also high in calcium and other micronutrients, such as vitamin K, vitamin B12, selenium and zinc.

Smoked salmon and asparagus

SERVES 1

Ingredients

9 asparagus spears

1 teaspoon olive oil

salt and pepper

3 slices smoked salmon

Method

1. Preheat oven to 180°C. Line a baking tray. Spread the asparagus spears across the tray and drizzle with olive oil and season with salt and pepper.

2. Bake for 8–10 minutes, or until the asparagus spears are crisp at the tips.

3. To serve, add 3 spears of asparagus to each slice of salmon and roll up.

HEALTH FACT

Asparagus are a great addition to a meal. They are rich in potassium that lowers blood pressure, and are low in calories and high in fibre, making them an excellent choice for health weight loss.

Sarah's chilli scrambled eggs with fetta

SERVES 1

Ingredients

1 teaspoon olive oil

2 eggs

1 birdseye chilli, seeds removed, finely chopped

25 grams chopped Danish fetta

1 tablespoon chopped fresh parsley

sea salt and freshly ground black pepper

Method

1. Add olive oil to a frying pan over medium-high heat.

2. Whisk the eggs in a bowl, add most of the chilli, keeping a little aside for garnish, then pour into the pan.

3. Add the fetta and cook, stirring occasionally to scramble the egg mixture. Transfer to a plate.

4. Add the remainder of the chopped chilli. Garnish with freshly chopped parsley and season to taste.

 HEALTH FACT

Adding chilli to meals can help with your healthy weight-loss journey. Chilli speeds up the metabolism and helps with fat burning. Research shows that chilli can also reduce low-density lipoprotein (LDL), also known as 'bad' cholesterol. Chillies are also rich in vitamin C and antioxidants, giving more reasons to add to your meals.

THE
10:10
DIET

LUNCH

LUNCH

Lunch would have to be my favourite meal of the day. I always make sure I have something delicious and nutritious ready to go.

For the right lunch, make sure you have a palm-sized portion of protein – plant or animal – with around 1½ cups of salad or vegetables. This can be in the form of soups, stews or stir-fries.

Making sure there is always protein as part of the meal will keep you full throughout the afternoon, keeping your mood stable and allowing you to get on with what you are doing without looking for a snack not long after.

Flavour is so important. You will notice in a lot of my recipes I use herbs and spices to garnish as well as nuts. I truly believe food should be delicious, especially when you're doing weight loss.

I am going to share with you some great tips for lunches on the go. The key to success is preparation. This is something I still do now, regardless of being at my goal weight for all my adult life.

Here are some of my favourite lunches to keep you inspired on your journey to health and wellness.

Beetroot, cheese and lentil salad

SERVES 2

Ingredients

2 beetroot, trimmed

1 cup baby spinach

¾ cup cooked lentils (or use canned lentils, drained)

50 grams cheddar cheese, diced

¼ cup chopped chives and parsley

2 tablespoons chopped roasted nuts

Dressing

1 clove garlic, crushed

1 tablespoon apple cider vinegar

1 tablespoon olive oil

½ teaspoon honey

½ teaspoon Dijon mustard

salt and pepper

Method

1. Preheat oven to 180°C. Line a baking tray. Chop the beetroot into wedges and bake for 30 minutes, until tender. Remove and let cool.

2. To assemble, arrange the spinach, lentils, beetroot, cheddar cheese and fresh herbs in a shallow bowl or on a plate. Sprinkle with chopped nuts.

3. Add the dressing ingredients to a bowl or jar and mix well, season to taste. Drizzle over the salad and serve.

 HEALTH FACT

Beetroot is rich in nitrates, which increase blood flow to the brain resulting in improved cognitive function. They are also great for your weight-loss journey. One serving of beetroot has only 44 calories.

Sarah's salmon frittata

SERVES 4

Ingredients

6 eggs

1½ cups almond flour

2 cups chopped spinach

200 grams smoked salmon

½ cup grated cheddar cheese

¼ cup olive oil

salt and pepper

Method

1. Preheat oven to 180°C. Grease a baking dish, around 20 cm x 30 cm and 3 cm deep.

2. Whisk the eggs in a bowl. Add the almond flour and blend with a wooden spoon. Add remaining ingredients, season to taste and combine.

3. Pour the egg mixture into the baking dish and cook for 25 minutes.

 HEALTH FACT

Almond flour is rich in vitamin E and other antioxidants, which may reduce the risk of serious diseases, such as diabetes, stroke, heart disease and cancer. Almond flour is also an excellent choice for a gluten-free diet.

Sarah's salmon poke bowl

SERVES 1

Ingredients

½ **cup cooked quinoa**

80 grams diced salmon

½ **cup shredded carrot**

½ **cup shredded beetroot**

¼ **avocado, sliced**

¼ **cup corn kernels**

½ **cup chopped spinach**

1 **teaspoon pickled ginger**

1 **tablespoon chopped spring onion**

1 **teaspoon black sesame seeds**

Poke sauce

2 teaspoons tamari

2 teaspoons sesame oil

1 **lemon, juiced**

**chopped chilli or chilli flakes
(to tolerance)**

Method

1. Spoon the quinoa into a bowl. Using the quinoa as the base, assemble the other ingredients in groups over the top of the quinoa. Sprinkle with sesame seeds.

2. Combine sauce ingredients in a bowl or jar, mix well and drizzle over the poke bowl.

Quinoa is an easily digested, super healthy grain. It is rich in protein, magnesium and copper, and has a low glycaemic index giving a slow release of energy after eating. It is a great gluten-free alternative to starchy grains.

Sarah's immune-boosting bowl

SERVES 1

Ingredients

½ cup broccoli florets

½ cup baby spinach

½ cup chopped capsicum

½ cup chopped beetroot

100 grams shredded chicken breast (poached or baked)

1 tablespoon chopped almonds and sunflower seeds

2 teaspoons olive oil

squeeze of lemon

salt and pepper

¼ cup chopped coriander

Method

1. Combine broccoli, spinach, capsicum, beetroot and chicken in a bowl.

2. Top with chopped almonds and sunflower seeds and drizzle with oil and lemon juice. Season to taste.

3. Sprinkle with chopped coriander for some extra immunity-boosting deliciousness.

 HEALTH FACT

Adding sunflower seeds to a meal will enhance your intake of vitamin E and antioxidants. The plant compounds in sunflower seeds are excellent for lowering inflammation.

Sarah's strawberry and chicken salad with mixed roasted nuts and strawberry dressing

SERVES 2

Ingredients

½ **cup mixed nuts (cashew, almond, macadamia, brazil, peanut)**

1½ **cups chopped fresh strawberries**

3 **cups mixed lettuce leaves**

½ **cup fresh basil leaves**

I **cup shredded cooked chicken breast**

Strawberry vinaigrette

½ **cup strawberries**

½ **lemon, juiced**

⅓ **tablespoon olive oil**

2 **tablespoons balsamic vinegar**

sea salt and freshly ground black pepper

Method

1. To dry roast the nuts, preheat oven to 180°C. Spread the nuts on a baking tray and roast for 10 minutes. Allow to cool.

2. Combine the ingredients for the salad (except nuts) in a bowl and toss.

3. For the vinaigrette, blitz the strawberries with the lemon juice until they are a purée.

4. In a jar, add the strawberry purée, olive oil and balsamic and shake really well. Add sea salt and pepper and shake again well. (An easy cheat's way is to just add 2 tablespoons of strawberry jam to the olive oil and vinegar.)

5. Toss the vinaigrette through the salad and drizzle the remainder over the top. Garnish with the roasted nuts.

Sarah's red cabbage, spinach and beetroot salad

SERVES 2

Ingredients

2½ cups grated beetroot

2 cups baby spinach leaves

1 cup grated red cabbage

1 cup grated carrot

10 chopped pecans, to garnish

1 bunch flat parsley, chopped,
  to garnish

Sarah's simple dressing

1 tablespoon olive oil

1 tablespoon apple cider vinegar

sea salt and freshly ground
  black pepper

Method

1. Assemble the beetroot, spinach, cabbage and carrot in a salad bowl, sprinkle with pecans and parsley.

2. Put the ingredients of the salad dressing in a tightly sealed jar and shake it ready to serve.

HEALTH FACT

Olive oil contains disease-fighting compounds. One of these compounds is oleocanthal, which causes the peppery sensation at the back of the throat when sipped neat. Oleocanthal reduces the inflammation caused by arthritis, helps fight and prevent cancer, and can slow down the progression of Alzheimer's disease.

Sarah's strawberry and bocconcini salad

SERVES 2

Ingredients

2 cups mixed greens

I punnet strawberries, chopped

I cup bocconcini balls

2 tablespoons chopped toasted almonds

Sarah's dressing

2 tablespoons extra-virgin olive oil

2 tablespoons balsamic vinegar

I teaspoon honey

¼ teaspoon sea salt

pinch of freshly ground pepper

Method

1. Place greens on a plate, add strawberries, bocconcini and almonds.

2. Put the ingredients of the salad dressing in a tightly sealed jar and shake it ready to serve.

HEALTH FACT

Bocconcini are small balls of fresh mozzarella made from the curd of buffalo and cow's milk. It is rich in calcium, iron, phosphorus, vitamin A and vitamin B. It has 25 per cent less fat than cheddar cheese.

Sarah's broccoli and flaxseed salad

SERVES 3

Ingredients

6 cups chopped broccoli

½ cup pumpkin seeds

¼ cup finely chopped red onion

2 tablespoons whole flaxseed

Dressing

½ cup yoghurt

2 tablespoons olive oil

2 tablespoons lemon juice

2 teaspoons honey

salt and pepper

Method

1. Combine broccoli, pumpkin seeds, onion and flaxseed in a large bowl.

2. In another bowl, combine yoghurt, olive oil, lemon juice and honey. Season to taste and mix well. Refrigerate before serving. Pour over salad, toss well.

 HEALTH FACT

Broccoli packs one of the most nutritional punches of any vegetable. It is excellent for heart health, contains cancer-protecting compounds, may be good for eye health, supports hormonal balance and with antioxidant properties, protects the body's cells from inflammatory damage.

Healthy protein salad with chicken, broccoli and quinoa

SERVES 2

Ingredients

½ brown onion, chopped

1 chicken breast

3 cups chicken stock

1 cup water

¾ cup quinoa

100 grams peas

1 head broccoli, cut into florets

1 tablespoon chopped fresh continental parsley

1 tablespoon chopped fresh chives

1 tablespoon shelled pistachios

½ tablespoon extra-virgin olive oil

1 tablespoon balsamic vinegar

salt and freshly ground black pepper

1 tablespoon pomegranate seeds

Method

1. Combine the chopped onion, chicken breast, 1 cup chicken stock plus 1 cup water. Bring to the boil over high heat. Reduce heat to low and simmer for 15 minutes, until the chicken is cooked through. Remove the chicken, shred, and set aside to cool.

2. Combine 2 cups chicken stock with ¾ cup quinoa in a pot. Bring to the boil, reduce heat to low, cover and simmer for 12 minutes, until all the water absorbs. Set aside to cool. Strain the quinoa before serving.

3. The peas and broccoli just need to be cooked until they are still crisp, we don't want them soggy for this salad. Drop the peas and chopped broccoli florets into boiling water for 2 minutes, remove and run under cold water straight away.

4. Combine the shredded chicken, peas, broccoli, parsley, chives, quinoa and pistachios in a bowl.

5. Combine the olive oil and vinegar in another bowl or jar and stir through the salad. Season with salt and freshly ground black pepper and top with pomegranate seeds.

Prawn, broccoli, fetta and roasted almond salad

SERVES 2

Ingredients

1 head broccoli, chopped into florets

20 roasted almonds

12 cooked, peeled prawns

75 grams fetta

½ cup chopped dill

Dressing

1 tablespoon olive oil

2 teaspoons honey

2 lemons, zested and juiced (set aside the zest to dress at the end)

Method

1. Blanch the broccoli in boiling water for 2 minutes, remove and run under cold water straight away.

2. Crush the almonds. (I do this by putting them in a sandwich bag and rolling over a rolling pin.)

3. For the dressing, combine the olive oil, honey and lemon juice in a jar or small bowl.

4. Assemble the broccoli and prawns on plates. Add the crushed almonds and fetta. Drizzle the dressing over the top, and sprinkle with dill and lemon zest.

HEALTH FACT

Prawns are a rich source of selenium, one of the most effective antioxidants to support the immune system and maintain healthy cells. They are also a rich source of iron, which helps in boosting the production of red blood cells.

Winter curry

SERVES 6

Ingredients

3 tablespoons sesame oil

½ teaspoon cumin

½ teaspoon turmeric

6 cloves garlic, chopped

1 tablespoon grated fresh ginger

chilli (cayenne or birdseye), to taste

1 brown onion, diced

salt and pepper

2 tablespoons tomato paste

1 cup diced pumpkin

1 parsnip, chopped

3 cups vegetable broth

1 cup cooked chickpeas

2 cups chopped cauliflower

1 bunch coriander

Optional: Greek yoghurt, to serve

Method

1. In a soup pot over medium heat, add the oil, cumin, turmeric, garlic, ginger and chilli. Stir well. Add the onion, salt and pepper, and cook until transparent.

2. Add the tomato paste, pumpkin, parsnip and vegetable broth. Bring to the boil. Reduce to a simmer. Cook for about 10–15 minutes or until the vegetables are cooked through. Add the chickpeas and cauliflower and cook for another 6 minutes. Add half a bunch of coriander and stir through.

3. Season with salt and pepper (if needed). Serve with Greek yoghurt, if using, and top with the remaining coriander.

Tofu sandwich

SERVES 1

Ingredients

100 grams firm tofu

**2 leaves cos or butter lettuce
(as the bread substitute)**

½ teaspoon Dijon mustard

1 tomato, sliced

3 small slices red onion

¼ cup rocket

Tofu marinade

½ teaspoon sesame oil

1 tablespoon tamari

1 teaspoon rice vinegar

1 teaspoon grated fresh ginger

Method

1. To prepare the marinade, combine the sesame oil, tamari, vinegar and ginger in a bowl and mix well.

2. Cut the tofu into palm-sized pieces and soak in the marinade for about an hour in the refrigerator.

3. Lay one lettuce leaf down and spread with mustard. Add the tomato, onion and rocket. Remove the tofu from the fridge, pat it down well, and add to the sandwich.

4. Place the other lettuce leaf on top and cut in the shape of a sandwich. Easy and delicious.

Eggplant burger

SERVES 2

Ingredients

½ eggplant

2 meat patties (see recipe below)

2 lettuce leaves

½ tomato, sliced

2 slices cheese

¼ red onion, sliced

2 pickles, sliced

salt and pepper

Method

1. Preheat oven to 180°C. Slice the eggplant into 4 discs about 1 cm thick. Place on a lined baking tray and cook for 12 minutes, turning halfway.

2. While the eggplant is cooking, cook the meat patties in a frying pan over high heat until cooked through.

3. Simply assemble as you would a regular burger. Place one eggplant disc on a plate, top with lettuce, tomato, meat patty, cheese, onion and pickle. Season to taste and top with the other eggplant disc.

Easy meat patties

SERVES 2

Ingredients

200 grams lean beef mince

1 egg

salt and pepper

Method

I keep this simple as I find when I add other ingredients it can fall apart. Simply add the egg to the mince and scrunch well to combine, add salt and pepper, then form two patties and pan fry for about 2 minutes each side. Simple.

Stuffed zucchini boats

SERVES 1

Ingredients

1 large zucchini, halved lengthwise

1 teaspoon olive oil

1 clove garlic, crushed

½ cup halved cherry tomatoes

1 tablespoon chopped fresh basil

½ chicken breast, shredded

salt and pepper

1 tablespoon shredded cheese

Method

1. Preheat oven to 190°C and line a baking tray. Hollow out the fleshy part of the zucchini so it resembles a canoe.

2. In a frying pan, add the olive oil, garlic, tomato, zucchini flesh, basil and chicken. Season to taste. Give it a good mix over low heat for a few minutes.

3. Add this mixture to the zucchini shells and top with the cheese. Bake for 15–17 minutes or until golden brown on top.

Smoked salmon and garden salad

SERVES 1

Ingredients

1 cup chopped iceberg lettuce

1 tablespoon chopped red onion

5 cherry tomatoes, halved

1 small cucumber, chopped

¼ capsicum, chopped

120 grams smoked salmon

¼ avocado, sliced

1 teaspoon olive oil

½ lemon, juiced

salt and pepper

Method

1. Add lettuce, onion, tomato, cucumber and capsicum to a bowl. Top with the smoked salmon and avocado.

2. Drizzle with olive oil, add lemon juice, and season to taste.

HEALTH FACT

Tomatoes are rich in an antioxidant called lycopene, which may prevent or slow down the progression of some types of cancers. Lycopene may also help lower your risk of developing heart disease and offer some protection again sunburn.

Baked salmon and greens

SERVES 1

Ingredients

3 brussels sprouts, trimmed and halved

½ cup chopped broccoli florets

1 small zucchini, sliced

120 grams salmon fillet

1 teaspoon olive oil

½ lemon, juiced

salt and pepper

1 teaspoon chopped fresh parsley

Method

1. Preheat the oven 180°C. Line a baking tray.

2. Assemble the vegetables on the baking tray around the salmon, drizzle with olive oil, and bake for 15–18 minutes or until the salmon is baked to your liking.

3. Transfer to a plate, add lemon juice, season to taste, and top with parsley.

HEALTH FACT

Lemon juice enhances the absorption of iron-rich foods, such as parsley.

Leek and mushroom omelette

SERVES 1

Ingredients

1 teaspoon olive oil

1 clove garlic, crushed

½ cup thinly sliced leek

½ cup chopped mushrooms

2 eggs, beaten

1 cup rocket, to serve

salt and pepper

Method

1. Heat the oil in a frying pan and add garlic, leek and mushrooms. Cook for a few minutes and set aside in a bowl.

2. Add the beaten eggs to the frying pan with a dash of olive oil. Add the cooked leek and mushroom mix onto one side of the eggs whilst in the frying pan.

3. Once the egg is cooked, flip over the other side of the egg mix to make a semi circle. Slide omelette onto a serving plate, add the rocket and serve with salt and pepper.

 HEALTH FACT

Leeks are rich in vitamin K, which may help reduce the risk of osteoporosis. They also contain carotenoids, which may reduce the risk of cataracts and macular degeneration.

ON-THE-GO
LUNCH IDEAS

ON-THE-GO LUNCH IDEAS

As I always say, the key to success is preparation. Skipping meals can result in poor food choices, you can end up too hungry and then overeating, and willpower is diminished.

Taking your lunch with you is always the best option. Organising your food will avoid food courts and cafes, but if you are faced with that as the only option, there are always choices you can make, such as going for sashimi or asking the sandwich bar to make you a bread-less sandwich or bun-less burger. There is always a solution.

Another tip is to cook a bit of extra protein with dinner the night before to add to vegetables or a salad in the morning rush. I do this regularly.

When on the 10:10 Diet, I recommend doing your food prep three days in advance. Foods such as cans of tuna, cheddar cheese, pickles, cottage cheese and boiled eggs are all things you should always have on hand.

I am going to share some easy on-the-go lunch recipes. Investing in a lunchbox and some cute little containers for salad dressings is always a good idea.

And don't forget to pack your fork as well!

Tuna and Greek salad

SERVES 1

Ingredients

1 x 95-gram can tuna, drained

1 cup chopped lettuce

5 cherry tomatoes

1 cucumber, sliced

1 tablespoon chopped onion

5 olives

1 tablespoon crumbled fetta

Dressing

½ lemon, juiced

1 teaspoon olive oil

salt and pepper

Method

1. Combine tuna and salad ingredients in a lunchbox container.

2. Combine dressing ingredients in a small jar. Drizzle over the salad just before serving.

HEALTH FACT

Fetta contains more calcium than many other cheeses and contains important minerals for healthy bones and teeth. Fetta is also rich in phosphorus, which is excellent for osteoporosis prevention. Phosphorus also plays an important role in how the body uses fats and carbohydrates and is needed by the body to make protein for the growth and repair of tissue and cells.

Egg wrap on the go

SERVES 1

Ingredients

1 large lettuce leaf

¼ avocado

2 boiled eggs

½ tomato, sliced

2 slices onion

¼ capsicum, sliced

1 cucumber, halved lengthwise and chopped

Method

1. Pack ingredients in a container or lunchbox (don't forget to pack a knife).

2. Lay the lettuce leaf out, spread the avocado along as you would a spread. Peel the eggs and cut them into slices. Layer the other ingredients on top and roll up.

HEALTH FACT *Just one capsicum gives you 166 per cent of your daily value for vitamin C, which is important for not only immunity but also for the growth, development and repair of body tissues.*

Goat cheese and broccoli salad

SERVES 1

Ingredients

50 grams goat cheese, diced

5 pickles, chopped

chopped onion, to your taste

1 cup chopped spinach

1 cup chopped broccoli

½ capsicum, diced

Dressing

1 teaspoon olive oil

½ teaspoon Dijon mustard

1 lemon, juiced

salt and pepper

Method

Assemble the ingredients in your lunchbox, chopped up ready to go. Make up the dressing in a separate jar.

HEALTH FACT

Pickles are rich in vitamin K, which is important for bone health and blood clotting.

DINNER

DINNER

I've always believed that dinner is a meal that should be slightly smaller than lunch. Traditionally, most Western countries have made dinner the largest meal of the day as it is also usually the time that the family eats together.

Research has shown, however, that eating a smaller dinner and a larger lunch is the key to helping you lose weight.

My formula for serving sizes for the 10:10 Diet journey is to keep the portion size of protein to the size of your palm and then your salad or vegetables to three cupped handfuls.

Here are some of my favourite dinner recipes to enjoy.

Sarah's san choy bau

SERVES 2

Ingredients

200 grams mixed pork and veal mince (you can use whatever mince you like)

1 red capsicum, chopped

1 onion, chopped

1 clove garlic, chopped

sea salt and freshly ground black pepper

2 tablespoons hoisin sauce (see recipe below)

1 iceberg or cos lettuce

Method

1. Cook the mince in a non-stick frying pan over medium heat until separated and brown. Add capsicum, onion and garlic. Season to taste.

2. Add the hoisin sauce, reduce heat and simmer for 10 minutes. Let the mince cool.

3. Gently separate the lettuce leaves so they remain intact and cut them to resemble bowls. Add the cooled mince mixture and serve.

Sarah's healthy twist on hoisin

Ingredients

2 tablespoons tamari or soy sauce

1 tablespoon good-quality smooth peanut butter

¼ teaspoon chilli powder

1 tablespoon sesame oil

1 tablespoon white vinegar

1 teaspoon honey

pinch of black pepper

1 clove garlic, crushed

Method

Mix all ingredients in a bowl to form a paste ready to add to the mince in the pan.

Sarah's stuffed mushrooms

SERVES 2

Ingredients

2 large field mushrooms

½ white onion, diced

1 tablespoon olive oil, for frying

1 cup chopped spinach

½ cup grated zucchini

2 eggs

120 grams ricotta

pinch of salt

1 tablespoon chopped parsley

1 tablespoon chopped chives

Method

1. Preheat oven to 180°C. Remove the mushroom stems from the mushrooms and chop stems. Scrape out the mushroom gills. Set aside the mushroom caps.

2. In a frying pan over medium heat, fry the onion in olive oil, then add the spinach, mushroom stems and zucchini. Let cool slightly.

3. Mix the eggs, ricotta and salt in a bowl. Add the cooked ingredients from the pan to the bowl and add the parsley and chives.

4. Lightly fry the mushroom caps on both sides.

5. Spoon the mixture into the mushroom caps, arrange on a baking tray, and bake in the oven for 25 minutes or until lightly browned.

Sarah's broccoli pizza

SERVES 4

Base

1 head broccoli, cut into florets

1 egg

⅓ cup almond flour

2 cloves garlic, crushed

½ cup grated mozzarella cheese

salt and pepper

Topping

1 cup shredded cheese

1 tomato, sliced

½ red onion, sliced

¼ cup fresh basil

¾ cup shredded cooked chicken breast

Method

1. Preheat oven to 200°C. Line a baking tray.

2. Blitz the broccoli to resemble rice in a food processor and then transfer to a tea towel and squeeze out as much water as possible.

3. In a bowl, combine the broccoli rice with the egg. Stir in almond flour, garlic, cheese, salt and pepper. Mix well.

4. Shape the broccoli mixture into a pizza-shaped circle about ½ cm high on the baking paper. Bake for 10–15 minutes or until golden brown. Remove from the oven.

5. Add the topping ingredients and bake for a further 8–10 minutes, or until golden brown.

Miso tofu

SERVES 2

Ingredients

250 grams firm tofu, sliced

½ cup mushrooms

1 cup chopped small yellow squash

1 bunch asparagus

1 tablespoon miso paste

1 tablespoon rice wine vinegar

1 cup rocket

1 cup chopped spinach or baby spinach

1 teaspoon sesame seeds

Method

1. Cook the tofu, mushrooms, squash and asparagus on a grill pan or barbecue for about 3 minutes each side.

2. Add the miso paste and rice wine vinegar to a bowl and mix well.

3. Place the rocket and spinach on a serving plate. Add the grilled tofu and vegetables. Drizzle the miso dressing over the top and sprinkle with sesame seeds.

HEALTH FACT

Squash is rich in beta-carotene, an antioxidant that may help slow down the progression of macular degeneration. It also supports eye health and prevents eye diseases. Squash is also rich in manganese that helps boost bone strength and the body's ability to process fats and carbohydrates. Miso paste is great for the immune system and digestion.

Sarah's cauliflower pizza

SERVES 4

Base

1 large cauliflower, trimmed

1 egg

¼ teaspoon dried oregano or mixed herbs

1 clove garlic, crushed

2 tablespoons grated parmesan cheese

pinch of sea salt

Topping

1 tablespoon tomato paste

200 grams protein of choice (such as smoked salmon, shredded chicken or tofu)

salt and pepper, to taste

1 handful baby spinach

120 grams fresh mozzarella, sliced

1 tablespoon grated parmesan cheese

Method

1. Preheat the oven to 180°C. Line a baking tray.

2. Blitz the cauliflower to resemble rice in a food processor. If you don't have one, use a cheese grater. Microwave or steam the cauliflower rice until really soft.

3. Put the hot cauliflower rice into a tea towel or cheese cloth and drain as much of the liquid out as possible. Squeeze a few times to be sure. (This step is really important.)

4. Put the drained rice in a mixing bowl, add the egg, dried oregano, garlic, grated parmesan cheese and salt and stir to combine.

5. Shape the cauliflower mixture into a pizza-shaped circle about ½ cm high on the baking paper. Bake for 10–15 minutes or until golden brown. Remove from the oven.

6. Add the tomato paste and toppings and bake for a further 8–10 minutes.

Bean and spinach stew

SERVES 2

Ingredients

1 tablespoon olive oil

1 red onion, chopped

2 cloves garlic, chopped

3 stalks celery, chopped

½ capsicum, chopped

1½ tablespoons tomato paste

1 cup chicken stock

1 cup chopped fresh tomatoes

1 zucchini, chopped

1 x 400-gram can cannellini beans

1 teaspoon dried dill

3 cups chopped spinach

salt and pepper, to taste

1 tablespoon fresh oregano

Method

1. Heat the oil in a frying pan and add onion, garlic, celery and capsicum. Cook for 5 minutes.

2. Add the tomato paste, chicken stock, tomatoes, zucchini, beans and dill. Bring to the boil then let simmer for 10 minutes. Add the spinach, simmer for a few minutes. Season to taste.

3. Sprinkle with fresh oregano to serve.

 HEALTH FACT

Cannellini beans, also known as white kidney beans, are a great source of calcium, iron and fibre. Beans are sometimes thought of as a carbohydrate food, but they contain little or no fat, making them a great addition to a low-fat diet. But watch out for the salt content as many canned beans are processed with high amounts of sodium. Try to use the low-salt variety.

Baked chicken breast and vegetables

SERVES 1

Ingredients

100 grams chicken breast

1 clove garlic, crushed

1 zucchini, sliced

½ cup broccoli

½ cup cauliflower

1 tomato, sliced

1 teaspoon olive oil

salt and pepper

1 teaspoon sunflower seeds

¼ cup chopped fresh coriander and parsley

Method

1. Preheat oven to 180°C. Line a baking tray.

2. Cut the chicken breast into thin strips and brush with garlic.

3. Place chicken breast and vegetables on the baking tray and drizzle with olive oil. Season to taste. Bake for 12 minutes.

4. Sprinkle with sunflower seeds, coriander and parsley to serve.

Ricotta eggplant

SERVES 4

Ingredients

1 eggplant

salt

500 grams ricotta

1 lemon, juiced

2 cloves garlic, chopped

1 tablespoon chopped fresh chives

1 tablespoon chopped fresh basil

salt and pepper

1 teaspoon olive oil

500 ml pasta sauce or passata

4 tablespoons mozzarella

1 tablespoon chopped fresh parsley,
to garnish

Method

1. Preheat oven to 160°C. Line a baking tray. Cut the eggplant lengthwise into slices 1 cm thick and lay the slices on the baking tray. Lightly salt in each side so the eggplant can dehydrate a bit.

2. Meanwhile, place the ricotta in a bowl and add the lemon juice, garlic, chives and basil; stir to combine. Add salt and pepper to taste and set aside in the refrigerator.

3. Pat down the eggplant with a paper towel. Lightly drizzle with olive oil. Bake for 10 minutes, turning over at 5 minutes. Remove from the oven. Increase oven temperature to 180°C.

4. Put a spoonful of ricotta mix on each eggplant slice and roll up to enclose the filling. Place in a baking dish. Place the rolls side by side, cover with pasta sauce, sprinkle with the mozzarella and bake for 20 minutes.

5. Garnish with fresh parsley. Enjoy with a green salad.

Cauliflower mash

SERVES 4

Ingredients

½ **head cauliflower, trimmed**

20 grams butter

1 tablespoon sour cream

sea salt and freshly ground black pepper

Optional: dash of milk

1 teaspoon chopped chives, to garnish

parsley, to garnish

Method

1. Steam the cauliflower until it is really soft.

2. Mash the old-fashioned way or put in the food processor; add the butter, sour cream, salt and pepper and combine to the consistency of mash; at this stage add the milk if required.

3. Garnish with chives and parsley. Serve as a side dish.

HEALTH FACT

Cauliflower is a fabulously healthy vegetable that contains unique plant compounds that may help reduce the risk of heart disease and cancer. Just one cup will give you 77 per cent of your recommended daily intake of vitamin C and 20 per cent of your recommended daily intake of vitamin K, which is needed to help keep calcium in bones. And one cup has only 25 calories.

Roasted broccoli and prawns

SERVES 2

Ingredients

1 head broccoli

2 tablespoons olive oil

1 teaspoon chopped birdseye chilli

salt and pepper

8 cooked, peeled prawn

1 lemon, for zest and wedges

1 bunch coriander, to garnish

Method

1. Preheat oven to 200°C. Toss the broccoli in a bowl with 1 tablespoon olive oil, chilli, salt and pepper.

2. In another bowl, combine the prawns with 1 tablespoon oil, lemon zest, salt and pepper.

3. Line a baking tray and spread the broccoli and prawns over the tray. Bake for 10 minutes and serve with the lemon wedges. Garnish with coriander.

 HEALTH FACT

Prawns are a source of iron, which helps in the production of red blood cells. They also contain calcium and selenium, which is important for thyroid health, supporting the immune system and for reproduction.

Prawn, avocado and lettuce cups

SERVES 1

Ingredients

6 cooked, peeled prawns, chopped

1 tablespoon yoghurt

½ teaspoon chopped fresh dill

¼ avocado, chopped

½ red capsicum, finely chopped

salt and pepper, to taste

2 iceberg lettuce leaves

Method

1. Mix the prawns, yoghurt, dill, avocado, capsicum, salt and pepper in a bowl.

2. Spoon the mixture into two lettuce cups and enjoy.

 HEALTH FACT

Iceberg lettuce is low in calories, sugar and fat. It has only about one calorie per lettuce leaf. It has a high water content making it a great choice for a hot summer's day. And it also provides calcium, potassium, vitamin C and folate.

Salmon patties

SERVES 4 (MAKES 8 PATTIES)

Ingredients

500 grams fresh salmon

2 teaspoons olive oil (one for the patty mix, one for cooking the salmon)

salt and pepper

1 brown onion, chopped

2 cloves garlic, chopped

½ cup almond flour

1 capsicum, diced

2 eggs, beaten

2 tablespoons good-quality mayonnaise

1 tablespoon Dijon mustard

2 tablespoons fresh dill

2 tablespoons olive oil (for cooking the patties)

Yoghurt and dill sauce

2 tablespoons good-quality Greek yoghurt

1 tablespoon chopped dill

⅛ teaspoon vanilla extract

Method

1. Preheat oven to 200°C. Cook the salmon with 1 teaspoon olive oil, salt and pepper in a frying pan over medium heat for about 10 minutes. Remove and let cool.

2. Add 1 teaspoon oil, onion, garlic, almond flour, capsicum, eggs, mayonnaise, mustard and dill to a bowl and mix well. Season to taste. Add the cooked salmon to combine into patties.

3. Add 2 tablespoons olive oil to a frying pan. Spoon the patty mixture into the pan, cooking in batches if needed. Cook each side over medium-high heat until golden brown.

4. Serve with the yoghurt and dill sauce.

Tuna patties

SERVES 3 (MAKES 6 PATTIES)

Ingredients

2 x 185-gram cans tuna

3 eggs

1 tablespoon lemon juice

½ cup red onion, diced

1 teaspoon chopped parsley

½ teaspoon chopped dill

2 cloves garlic, chopped

pinch of salt and pepper

olive oil, for cooking

Method

1. Blend all ingredients, except olive oil, in a bowl until well combined.

2. Heat the oil in a frying pan over medium heat. Divide patty mixture into tablespoon-sized balls, flatten to patties, and fry each side until golden brown.

3. Enjoy the patties on their own or serve with a salad.

HEALTH FACT

Tuna is packed with omega-3, vitamins B12 and D, calcium and iron. Just 85 grams of canned tuna gives you almost 50 per cent of your recommended daily intake for vitamin D. We need vitamin D for our immunity, energy levels, growth, calcium uptake and mood. Canned tuna is often a concern to people because of the mercury content it contains. My guidelines are to have canned tuna once or twice a week, at around 90 grams per serve.

Sarah's salmon and pesto zucchini noodles

SERVES 2

Ingredients

1 large salmon fillet

1–2 tablespoons olive oil (to cook salmon)

salt and pepper

2 large zucchini

1 teaspoon olive oil (to cook zucchini noodles)

½ small lemon

Sarah's pesto

1½ cups chopped spinach

½ cup shelled pistachios

2 cloves garlic

2 tablespoons extra-virgin olive oil

1 cup parsley leaves

½ cup grated parmesan cheese

1 lemon, juiced

sea salt and pepper

Method

1. Preheat oven to 200°C. Brush the salmon with olive oil and sprinkle with salt and pepper. Bake on a lined baking tray for 12–15 minutes.

2. Meanwhile, combine pesto ingredients in a blender or food processor and process until smooth.

3. Cut the ends off the zucchini. Create noodles with a spiraliser. If you don't have one you can use a potato peeler.

4. In a frying pan, add olive oil over medium heat. Add zucchini noodles and cook for about 2 minutes until noodles have just begun to soften. Remove from heat and add pesto, tossing the zucchini noodles so they're evenly coated.

5. Remove salmon from the oven, break into small pieces and toss through the noodles. Enjoy!

Seared tuna and wasabi

SERVES 2

Ingredients

1 teaspoon wasabi

2 tablespoons olive oil

1 lime, juiced

1 teaspoon mirin

2 x 120-gram tuna steaks

1 tablespoon tamari

1 clove garlic, crushed

2 teaspoons sesame oil

1 cup snow peas

1 cucumber, thinly sliced

2 red radishes, as thinly sliced as possible

2 teaspoons black sesame seeds, toasted

Method

1. To make the wasabi dressing, combine the wasabi, olive oil, lime juice and mirin in a bowl or jar.

2. Toss the tuna in a bowl with the tamari, garlic and sesame oil. In a frying pan over high heat, cook the tuna until lightly seared, about 2 minutes each side.

3. Combine the snow peas, cucumber and radishes in a bowl.

4. Slice the seared tuna and serve with the salad. Drizzle wasabi dressing over the top. Top with black sesame seeds for decoration.

Fish curry

SERVES 2

Ingredients

1 tablespoon olive oil

½ onion, chopped

2 cloves garlic, chopped

2 green chillies, chopped

1 tablespoon grated fresh ginger

1 teaspoon turmeric

1 teaspoon curry powder

1 teaspoon cumin

1 cup fish stock

200 ml almond milk

300 grams barramundi

½ head cauliflower, chopped

coriander, to garnish

Method

1. Add olive oil, onion, garlic, chillies, ginger, turmeric, curry powder and cumin to a pot and cook over medium heat for a few minutes.

2. Add the fish stock and milk and cook for about 10 minutes while the flavours blend. Add the fish and cook for a further 5 minutes.

3. Meanwhile, add chopped cauliflower to a food processor and process until it resembles rice. Microwave it in a glass bowl for 5 minutes.

4. Serve cauliflower rice as the base, with the fish curry and some coriander chopped over the top.

Chicken and pear salad

SERVES 2

Ingredients

1 chicken breast

1 cup rocket

1 cup spinach

½ red onion, chopped

½ pear, sliced

2 tablespoons sunflower and
   pumpkin seeds

50 grams Danish fetta

1 tablespoon balsamic vinegar

2 teaspoons olive oil

salt and pepper, to taste

Method

1. Cook the chicken. You can poach, grill, bake or pan-fry the chicken, or use a barbecue chicken. Shred when cooked.

2. Assemble the salad ingredients in a bowl including the olive oil and balsamic vinegar and toss well.

3. Add the shredded chicken and enjoy.

HEALTH FACT

Pears are a powerhouse fruit packed with vitamins, fibre and beneficial plant compounds. Don't peel the pear as many of the fruit's nutrients are found in the skin. Pears complement chicken as well as cheese and can help keep you feeling full due to their high water content and fibre.

Chicken, strawberry and avocado salad

SERVES 2

Ingredients

1 chicken breast

1 teaspoon olive oil

1 cup chopped spinach

1 cup chopped rocket

250 grams strawberries, chopped

½ avocado, diced

Dressing

1 tablespoon balsamic vinegar

1 tablespoon olive oil

salt and pepper

Method

1. Rub the chicken breast with oil. Cook in a frying pan over high heat, until golden brown on each side.

2. Place the spinach, rocket and chopped strawberries in a bowl.

3. Thinly slice the chicken breast and place in the bowl. Add the diced avocado to the top of the salad.

4. Drizzle the dressing ingredients over the top of the salad and serve.

HEALTH FACT

Spinach is packed with carotenoids, vitamin C, vitamin K, folic acid, iron and calcium. It benefits eye health, may help prevent cancer and can help reduce high blood pressure levels. Rocket is high in vitamin C and vitamin K. Eat it to boost immunity and help keep bones healthy.

Almond and cashew-crusted barramundi

SERVES 2

Ingredients

1 teaspoon butter

1 tablespoon olive oil

½ cup almonds and cashews, chopped up well

2 teaspoons chopped parsley

2 x 120-gram pieces of barramundi

1 lemon, cut into wedges

Garden salad

2 cups salad greens

½ capsicum, chopped

1 teaspoon chopped red onion

1 cucumber, chopped

5 cherry tomatoes

salt and pepper, to taste

1 lemon, juiced

1 teaspoon olive oil

Method

1. Preheat oven to 180°C. Melt butter and olive oil in a frying pan.

2. Assemble the chopped nuts and parsley on a plate. Dip the fish in the pan with the melted oil and butter mixture then into the nut mix. Press the nuts firmly into the fish.

3. Line a baking tray and bake the fish for 10 minutes, or until the fish is cooked through.

4. While the fish is cooking, assemble the garden salad in a bowl or on a plate then add the fish. Enjoy.

Chicken skewers and Greek salad

SERVES 2

Ingredients

1 tablespoon olive oil

1 lemon, juiced

1 clove garlic, crushed

1 teaspoon oregano

pinch of cinnamon

¼ teaspoon paprika

1 chicken breast, chopped

Greek salad

1 large or 2 small cucumbers, diced

10 cherry tomatoes

¼ red onion, chopped

1 iceberg lettuce, roughly chopped

50 grams fetta

Dressing

1 lemon, juiced

1 teaspoon olive oil

salt and pepper, to taste

Method

1. Combine the oil, lemon juice, garlic, oregano, cinnamon and paprika in a glass bowl. Add the chopped chicken, cover and refrigerate for 1 hour to marinate.

2. Thread the chicken pieces onto skewers and cook under the grill or on a barbecue for 8–10 minutes or until cooked through.

3. Combine the salad ingredients in a bowl and add dressing. Serve with the chicken skewers.

Easy chicken roast

SERVES 2

Ingredients

1 tablespoon olive oil

zest of 1 lemon

2 cloves garlic, crushed

2 teaspoons dried oregano

2 thyme sprigs

1 teaspoon chilli flakes

salt and pepper, to taste

4 skinless chicken thighs

250 grams cherry tomatoes

Method

1. Preheat oven to 200°C. Combine the oil, lemon zest, garlic, oregano, thyme, chilli, salt and pepper in a glass bowl. Add the chicken and turn to coat. Cover and refrigerate for 30 minutes to marinate.

2. Spread the chicken on a baking tray and roast for about 30 minutes. Add the tomatoes and roast for a further 10 minutes.

HEALTH
FACT

Cherry tomatoes are loaded with vitamins and minerals. They are a great source of lycopene, which can help with blood clotting so may help prevent strokes. They also contain compounds that are associated with lowering the risk of many diseases, including cancer. For men, eating cherry tomatoes may reduce your risk of prostate cancer.

Chicken cacciatore

SERVES 2

Ingredients

2 tablespoons olive oil

4 skinless chicken thighs

1 onion, chopped

2 cloves garlic, chopped

½ cup olives

1 capsicum, chopped

1 teaspoon dried rosemary

425 grams fresh tomatoes, chopped

salt and pepper

¼ cup chopped parsley

Method

1. Heat 1 tablespoon oil in a frying pan over medium-high heat. Cook the chicken until golden brown on each side. Set aside. Add 1 tablespoon oil, onion and garlic to the pan and cook until translucent.

2. Add the olives, capsicum, rosemary and chopped tomatoes to the pan and cook for 10 minutes. Return the chicken to the pan, reduce heat to low, and simmer until the chicken is cooked through, about 20 minutes. Season to taste.

3. Serve with chopped parsley.

HEALTH FACT

Rosemary is a herb that is a member of the mint family. It is native to the Mediterranean and has many health benefits. It is a rich source of antioxidants and anti-inflammatory compounds, which help boost the immune system, improve blood circulation, help digestion and improve concentration. It is also an excellent source of iron, calcium and vitamin B6.

Easy beef stew

SERVES 6

Ingredients

1 kg diced beef

salt and pepper

1 tablespoon olive oil

1 medium onion, chopped

2 cloves garlic, chopped

2 carrots, chopped

3 stalks celery, chopped

1 litre beef stock

2 bay leaves

1 x 425-gram can tomatoes

1 teaspoon dried basil

1 teaspoon dried parsley

fresh parsley, to serve

Method

1. Season the diced beef. In a frying pan over medium heat, sear the diced meat in the olive oil until browned.

2. Add the onion and garlic and continue to cook until the onion is translucent. Stir in carrots and celery and cook for 4–5 minutes until tender.

3. Add remaining ingredients and bring to the boil, then let simmer for about 50 minutes.

4. Serve with fresh parsley.

HEALTH FACT

Beef stock is easy to digest and is packed with nutrients and amino acids, which are important for growth. Beef stock is low in calories and high in gelatin so is excellent for bone health, strengthening hair and nails, healing any wounds along the digestive tract, reducing inflammation and can even help with sleep due to its magnesium content.

Beef and vegetables

SERVES 2

Ingredients

200 grams diced beef

2 teaspoons olive oil

1 onion, sliced

2 cloves garlic, crushed

½ capsicum, chopped

⅓ cup water

1 carrot

1 cup chopped cauliflower

1 cup zucchini

1 cup chopped asparagus

1 tablespoon tamari

1 tablespoon honey

¼ cup fresh parsley

Method

1. Slice the beef dice into strips and add to a frying pan with 1 teaspoon of olive oil over high heat and cook until golden brown. Set aside to rest.

2. Add the other teaspoon of olive oil to the frying pan. Add onion, garlic and capsicum and cook until the onion is translucent.

3. Add the water and the remaining vegetables and cook for 4–5 minutes until tender. Add the tamari and honey and stir through.

4. Place the beef on top of the vegetables and serve with a garnish of fresh parsley.

 HEALTH FACT

Honey has been used as a folk remedy throughout history and has a variety of health and medical benefits. It is even used in some hospitals to treat wounds. Honey is also a prebiotic that feeds the good bacteria in your gut, leading to a healthier digestive system. It also has antibacterial and antifungal properties and is a good source of antioxidants. But most health benefits relate to raw honey, not the pasteurised honey you find in supermarkets. You can buy raw honey from health food shops or local suppliers.

Steamed vegetables and pork cutlet

SERVES 1

Ingredients

1 pork cutlet (100 grams)

½ cup chopped carrot

½ cup chopped cauliflower

½ cup broccoli florets

chopped herbs, to garnish

Method

1. Grill the pork chop until cooked through, about 2–3 minutes each side.

2. Lightly steam the carrot, cauliflower and broccoli in a steamer for a few minutes.

3. Serve with a garnish of chopped herbs.

 HEALTH FACT

Pork is an excellent source of vitamins and minerals and is high in protein. Unlike other red meats, pork is rich in thiamine, or vitamin B1, which is required by our bodies to properly use carbohydrates and maintain nerve function. Pork is also abundant in zinc, which we need for immunity and brain health. Pork contains all nine essential amino acids needed for body growth and maintenance, so is beneficial to people who need to build up or repair muscle.

Mushroom burgers

SERVES 2

Ingredients

**2 burger patties
(see Easy meat patties recipe on
page 67 or buy good-quality lean
beef patties)**

4 portobello mushrooms

1 teaspoon butter

2 slices tomato

2 slices beetroot

½ avocado, sliced

1 carrot, shredded

½ cup chopped rocket

1 teaspoon chopped red onion

Method

1. Cook the meat patties in a frying pan over medium-high heat until browned. Set aside.

2. Remove the stems from the mushrooms and fry in butter for a few minutes until browned.

3. Simply assemble the burger. Starting with the mushroom as a base, stack the patty, tomato, beetroot, avocado, carrot and rocket on top, and then place the other mushroom on top. Hold it together with a toothpick and serve. Repeat for the second burger.

Sarah's super healthy lasagne

SERVES 6

Meat sauce

2 tablespoons olive oil

750 grams beef mince

1 onion, finely chopped

2 cloves garlic, chopped

1 carrot, shredded

5 tablespoons tomato paste

2 x 425-gram cans tomatoes

500 ml chicken stock

salt and pepper

White sauce

1 cauliflower, trimmed

1 litre vegetable stock

½ white onion, chopped

1 clove garlic, crushed

50 grams butter

salt and pepper

1–2 tablespoons milk

Sarah's super
healthy lasagne *continued*

SERVES 6

Layers

**4 zucchini, sliced lengthwise
about 2–3 mm thick**

5 cabbage leaves

**I cup grated cheese
(save ½ for the topping)**

Method

1. Preheat oven to 180°C. Heat oil in a large
    frying pan over medium heat. Add mince,
    breaking up lumps with a wooden spoon,
    and cook for 3–4 minutes or until browned.
    Add onion, garlic, carrot and tomato paste
    and cook for 10 minutes or until cooked
    through. Add tomatoes, chicken stock, salt
    and pepper and simmer for 20 minutes,
    then remove from heat and set aside.

2. Add cauliflower to a large saucepan with
    the vegetable stock. Cook for 10 minutes,
    or until the cauliflower is very soft.

3. Meanwhile, cook the onion and garlic in
    butter in a frying pan over medium heat until
    transparent. Combine the onion and garlic
    with the cooked cauliflower in a blender. Add
    salt and pepper and milk and blitz until it looks
    like a thick sauce.

4. To assemble the lasagne, spoon a first layer of
    meat sauce into a lightly greased baking dish,
    followed by a layer of zucchini, then the white
    sauce and a sprinkle of cheese. For the next
    layer, use the cabbage for your 'pasta sheet'
    layer, followed by the meat sauce, white sauce
    and a sprinkle of cheese, and repeat.

5. Sprinkle with ½ cup cheese as the topping.
    Bake for 30 minutes, until the top is golden
    brown. Delish!

Lamb backstrap and vegetables

SERVES 2

Ingredients

1 cup chopped broccolini

½ cup chopped small yellow squash

½ cup chopped brussels sprouts

2 teaspoons olive oil

200 grams lamb backstrap

¼ cup chopped mint

salt and freshly ground black pepper

Method

1. Add the vegetables to a hot frying pan with 1 teaspoon olive oil, and stir-fry them for about 5 minutes, until crisp.

2. In another frying pan, add 1 teaspoon olive oil over medium-high heat and cook the lamb backstrap for 3–4 minutes each side or to your liking. Set aside to rest. Slice.

3. Serve the lamb and vegetables garnished with chopped mint and a drizzle of olive oil. Season to taste.

Lamb and broccoli

SERVES 2

Ingredients

1 head broccoli

¼ cup pumpkin seeds

2 lamb steaks

1 teaspoon lemon zest

2 spring onions, chopped

1 red chilli, chopped

40 grams Danish fetta

2 teaspoons olive oil

2 tablespoons balsamic vinegar

1 clove garlic, crushed

Method

1. Preheat oven to 180°C. Roast the broccoli and pumpkin seeds on a baking tray for 15 minutes.

2. Cook the lamb steaks in a frying pan over medium-high heat for 5 minutes each side or to your liking. Add the lemon zest to the lamb. Set aside to rest.

3. Place the cooked broccoli in a bowl and mix in the spring onions, chilli and fetta.

4. Add the olive oil, balsamic vinegar and crushed garlic to a jar, shake well and pour over the broccoli.

HEALTH FACT

Lemon peel or zest has numerous health benefits. Just one tablespoon provides you with 9 per cent of your recommended daily value of vitamin C. Lemon zest also helps oral health due to its antibacterial properties that block the growth of microorganisms.

Lamb curry

SERVES 4

Ingredients

1 tablespoon olive oil

500 grams chopped lamb

1 tablespoon curry powder

1 onion, chopped

3 cloves garlic, chopped

250 ml coconut milk

1 cup water

salt, to taste

1 carrot, chopped

½ cup chopped cauliflower

1 cup broccoli florets

fresh mint, to serve

Method

1. Heat oil in a casserole dish over medium heat, add the lamb and brown in batches. Remove and set aside.

2. Add the curry powder, onion and garlic and cook until the onion is translucent.

3. Return the lamb to the casserole dish. Add coconut milk, water and salt and simmer for about 45 minutes.

4. Add the vegetables and cook, covered, for a further 30 minutes. Add the fresh mint at the end.

SOUPS

SARAH'S FAVOURITE SOUPS
FOR 10:10 DIET SUCCESS

I am yet to find someone who is not a soup lover. Nothing beats the deliciousness of a warm soup in winter. There are so many flavours to choose from, the world is your oyster when it comes to what type of soup you like.

If the soup recipe doesn't contain any legumes or animal protein, then add a palm-sized portion of protein to your soup or enjoy the protein on the side.

Adding yoghurt or cheese to your soup constitutes your protein requirement for your meal.

The guideline for cheese and yoghurt toppings is 2 tablespoons of yoghurt and about 50 grams of cheese. The serving size for the soup is 1 cup.

The soup would fall into the category of your serving size of vegetables for your meal.

Soups that contain legumes are a complete meal as legumes are a form of protein as well as a carbohydrate.

I hope you enjoy my favourite soups for the 10:10 Diet meal plan as much as I do.

Sarah's super creamy green weight-loss soup

SERVES 4

Ingredients

1 tablespoon olive oil

2 stalks celery

1 carrot, diced

1 parsnip, diced

1 yellow capsicum, diced

1 onion, diced

2 cloves garlic, chopped

1 tablespoon grated fresh ginger

4 cups vegetable broth

2 cups chopped spinach

1 head broccoli, chopped

1 tablespoon miso paste

sea salt and freshly ground black pepper

1 tablespoon yoghurt

chopped coriander, to serve

Method

1. Heat olive oil in a large pot over medium-high heat. Add celery, carrot, parsnip, capsicum, onion and garlic. Cook, stirring, until the onion and garlic is transparent, about 5 minutes.

2. Add ginger and vegetable broth, reduce heat to medium and add spinach and broccoli. Cook for about 20 minutes. Add miso paste and season to taste. Using a blender or handheld blender to blend until creamy.

3. Ladle the soup into bowls and serve with yoghurt on top. Garnish with chopped coriander.

Hearty lentil and white bean soup

SERVES 4

Ingredients

1 tablespoon oil

1 brown onion, diced

1 large carrot, peeled and diced

3 cloves garlic, crushed

3 sprigs fresh thyme

2 bay leaves

5 cups chicken stock

½ cup brown or red lentils

¼ cup dry white wine (add extra ¼ cup chicken stock for a non-alcoholic option)

sea salt and freshly ground black pepper

2 x 400-gram cans cannellini beans

1 x 425-gram can diced tomatoes

2 tablespoons chopped fresh parsley leaves

Optional: freshly grated parmesan cheese, to garnish

Method

1. Heat oil in a large stock pot over medium-high heat, add the onion and carrot, and cook, stirring occasionally, until the onion is translucent, about 4 minutes.

2. Add garlic, thyme and bay leaves. Stir for 1 minute.

3. Add chicken stock, lentils, wine if using, salt and pepper to taste.

4. Bring to the boil, cover, reduce heat to a simmer and cook until lentils are almost tender, about 15 minutes.

5. Rinse the cannellini beans under cold water and add to the soup. Add the tomatoes and cook for a further 10 minutes.

6. To serve, garnish with freshly chopped parsley and if desired, freshly grated parmesan cheese.

Broccoli, miso and pea soup

SERVES 4

Ingredients

2 tablespoons organic coconut oil

1 white onion, chopped

1 clove garlic, chopped

1 head broccoli, chopped

1 tablespoon chopped fresh ginger

3 cups frozen peas

¼ cup miso paste

500 ml water

500 ml vegetable stock

sea salt and freshly ground black pepper

Method

1. Heat the coconut oil in a frying pan over low heat, add onion and garlic and cook, stirring occasionally, until the onion is translucent (not browned), about 4 minutes.

2. Place all other ingredients in a deep saucepan, bring to the boil and then simmer for about 15 minutes.

3. Once the broccoli is tender, add the onion and garlic and blitz until smooth. It is absolutely delicious.

HEALTH FACT

Miso is made from fermented soybeans and is a staple in Asian cuisine. It is a great source of probiotics that help with digestion and gut health. It may also help reduce the risk of certain cancers, support the immune system and help with anxiety and depression.

Cauliflower soup

SERVES 4

Ingredients

1 large head cauliflower

2 tablespoons olive oil

pinch of salt

1 red onion, chopped

2 cloves garlic, chopped

1 litre vegetable stock

2 tablespoons butter

½ lemon, juiced

chopped parsley, chives and coriander, to garnish

pumpkin seeds, for sprinkling

Method

1. Preheat oven to 180°C. Chop the cauliflower into small pieces. Line a baking tray. Toss the cauliflower in 1 tablespoon olive oil, lightly salt and bake for about 25 minutes.

2. Heat 1 tablespoon oil in a large saucepan or soup pot over medium-high heat. Add onion and garlic and cook until translucent.

3. Add the cooked cauliflower and the vegetable stock to the pot. Bring to the boil, reduce heat and simmer for 20–25 minutes.

4. Set aside for a few minutes to cool slightly. Add the butter and lemon juice. Use a handheld blender in the pot or transfer to a blender. Blitz into a soup-like texture, season to taste.

5. Serve dressed with the herb mix and sprinkle some pumpkin seeds on top.

Sarah's super healthy chicken and vegetable soup

SERVES 8

Ingredients

1 tablespoon olive oil

1 onion, thinly sliced

2 cloves garlic, crushed

1 large carrot, diced

2 stalks celery, diced

2 zucchini, diced

8 cups chicken stock

1½ kg chicken thighs

1 cup soup mix

Optional: 2 stock cubes for extra flavour

salt and pepper

1 handful fresh parsley, chopped, to garnish

Method

1. Heat oil in a soup pot over medium heat. Add onion and garlic and cook until transparent. Add carrot, celery and zucchini and cook for a few more minutes. Add the stock, chicken and soup mix. Add crumbled stock cubes if using.

2. Bring to the boil and cook, covered, on low heat for about 1½ hours. Remove the chicken from the soup with a slotted spoon, remove the chicken meat from the bone and return the meat to the soup.

3. Season to taste and serve with parsley.

Tomato and turmeric soup

SERVES 2

Ingredients

I tablespoon olive oil

I medium-sized onion, chopped

2 cloves garlic, chopped

5 cups chopped ripe tomatoes

2 teaspoons turmeric powder

¾ cup vegetable stock

I tablespoon apple cider vinegar

pinch of sea salt

I teaspoon dried basil leaves

I tablespoon mixed seeds and nuts,
   to garnish

I handful parsley leaves, chopped,
   to garnish

Method

1. Heat oil in a frying pan over low heat, add onion and garlic and cook, stirring occasionally, until the onion is translucent.

2. Add the tomatoes and turmeric and cook until the tomatoes are really soft.

3. Transfer to a saucepan or soup pot.

4. Add vegetable stock, apple cider vinegar, salt and basil and bring to the boil. Simmer for 5–8 minutes. Then blitz in the pot with a handheld blender or transfer to a blender.

5. Top with nuts, seeds and chopped parsley to serve. Delish.

SOUPS

Spicy pumpkin soup

SERVES 4

Ingredients

1 red onion, sliced

3 cloves garlic, crushed

1 tablespoon olive oil

2 carrots, chopped

1 kg pumpkin, chopped

1 teaspoon chilli flakes

2 teaspoons ground coriander

1 litre chicken stock

½ cup milk

salt and pepper, to taste

Greek yoghurt, to serve

chopped fresh chilli, deseeded, to garnish

chopped fresh coriander, to garnish

Method

1. Add the onion and garlic to a saucepan with olive oil. Cook until translucent.

2. Add the carrot and pumpkin with chilli flakes and ground coriander. Cook until the pumpkin and carrot are slightly caramelised.

3. Add stock and bring to the boil, reduce heat and simmer until the carrots are cooked through. Add the milk, salt and pepper and blend in the pot using a handheld blender or transfer to a blender.

4. To serve, add a dollop of Greek yoghurt and garnish with fresh chilli and coriander.

Anti-inflammatory soup with turmeric, ginger and carrot

SERVES 4

Ingredients

1 onion, chopped

2 cloves garlic, chopped

1 tablespoon olive oil

4 medium carrots, chopped

1 tablespoon grated fresh ginger

1 tablespoon ground turmeric

1 litre vegetable stock

1 lemon, juiced

salt and pepper

2 teaspoons coconut yoghurt
per bowl

mixed seeds and chopped coriander,
to garnish

Method

1. Sauté the onion and garlic in olive oil, until translucent.

2. Add the carrot, ginger and turmeric and cook for another couple of minutes. Add the stock and lemon juice. Cook for about 20 minutes until the carrot is soft. Season to taste.

3. Divide into serving bowls, top each bowl with coconut yogurt and garnish with the seeds and coriander.

 HEALTH FACT

Turmeric is one of my favourite spices. Its active compound has many scientifically proven health benefits such as helping improve heart health, fighting inflammation and helping protect against diseases such as arthritis, cancer, cystic fibrosis and Alzheimer's disease.

Broccoli, zucchini and spinach soup

SERVES 4

Ingredients

½ kg broccoli (approx. 2 heads)

2 tablespoons olive oil

1 onion, chopped

2 cloves garlic, chopped

1 litre chicken stock

2 zucchini, chopped

4 cups chopped spinach

salt and pepper, to taste

1 tablespoon chopped parsley

1 tablespoon chopped dill

Method

1. Chop the broccoli into evenly sized pieces and add to a food processor or blender. Blitz until it resembles green grains of rice.

2. Heat the oil in a large saucepan or soup pot and cook the onion and garlic until transparent.

3. Add the chicken stock, zucchini, spinach and broccoli rice and cook for about 10 minutes over medium heat. Allow to cool slightly and blend in the pot with a handheld blender. Season to taste.

4. Divide into serving bowls and top with chopped parsley and dill.

Celery and leek soup

SERVES 4

Ingredients

2 cups chopped celery

2 cups chopped leek

2 cloves garlic, crushed

1 tablespoon tamari

750 ml vegetable stock

150 ml almond milk

salt and pepper

chopped parsley and chives, to garnish

Method

1. Add the celery, leek, garlic, tamari and vegetable stock to a saucepan and bring to the boil, reduce heat and simmer for 20 minutes.

2. Add the milk and blitz with a handheld blender until smooth.

3. Season to taste and serve with chopped parsley and chives.

HEALTH FACT

Celery has a high water content and is loaded with vitamins and minerals. It contains folate and vitamin K which are important for making red blood cells and for clotting. It also has a low glycaemic index so is great for people who have to monitor their blood sugar levels.

THE
10:10
DIET

DETOX

DETOX RECIPES

I love the detox section of the 10:10 Diet, primarily because I see a detox as a time to stop, reflect and show some self-love. Detox for me is far from anything that is depriving, punishing or unpleasant.

The basic foundations of the detox meals are:

- white proteins only (avoid red meat)
- no diary milk or yoghurt
- gluten free
- nothing artificial, processed or with any flavours or additives
- fresh vegetables
- fresh fruit
- clean real food, wholefood dietary principles
- no alcohol
- food cooked without burning – no barbecue or frying.

On the detox, I always get you to start the day with a nutrient-dense smoothie – they are wonderful for liver health to support the detoxification process.

Detox smoothie

SERVES 1

Ingredients

½ cup chopped spinach

½ cup chopped kale

2 stalks celery, chopped

1 kiwi fruit, chopped

1 tablespoon chia seeds

1 teaspoon grated fresh ginger

½ cup coconut yoghurt

1 dessertspoon nut butter (any nut butter without peanuts)

4 large ice cubes

½ cup water

Optional: 1 teaspoon honey

Method

Simply add the ingredients to a bullet blender, blitz and enjoy.

Rejuvenating detox smoothie

SERVES 1

Ingredients

½ cup halved strawberries

½ cup blueberries

1 cup chopped spinach

½ frozen banana

pinch of cinnamon

1 dessertspoon nut butter (any nut butter without peanuts)

4 ice cubes

½ cup water

Optional: 1 teaspoon honey

Method

Add ingredients to a bullet blender, blitz and enjoy.

Tofu and bok choy soup

SERVES 2

Ingredients

250 grams firm tofu, cubed

1 teaspoon grated fresh ginger

pinch of salt

1 cup water

2 teaspoons sesame oil

250 grams bok choy

Dipping sauce

3 green chillies, finely chopped

1 clove garlic, crushed

½ tablespoon tamari

pinch of salt

1 teaspoon honey

½ tablespoon sesame oil

Method

1. To prepare the dipping sauce, combine the chillies, garlic, tamari, salt and honey in a small bowl. Heat the sesame oil in a frying pan over low heat for a few minutes, then add to the sauce. Set aside.

2. In a pot, add the tofu, ginger, salt and water and bring to the boil, reduce heat; add the sesame oil and bok choy and cook for another minute.

3. Serve immediately with the dipping sauce on the side.

Detox salad

SERVES 1

Ingredients

½ cup blueberries

1 cup chopped spinach

1 cup chopped rocket

1 cucumber, chopped

½ cup grated beetroot

½ cup grated carrot

¼ avocado, sliced

Dressing

1 lemon, juiced

1 teaspoon sesame oil

1 teaspoon tahini

1 teaspoon honey

1 clove garlic, crushed

salt and pepper

Toppings

1 spring onion, chopped

1 tablespoon chia seeds

¼ cup chopped coriander

Method

1. Assemble the salad ingredients in sections in a shallow bowl.

2. Add the dressing ingredients to a jar and shake well.

3. Sprinkle the spring onion, chia seeds and coriander over the top of the salad. Serve with the dressing.

Detox soup

SERVES 4

Ingredients

½ **cup chopped leek**

3 **cloves garlic, chopped**

1 **tablespoon olive oil**

1 **head broccoli, chopped**

2 **zucchini, chopped**

1 **cup chopped spinach**

1 **litre vegetable stock**

salt and pepper

½ **cup coriander, to serve**

½ **cup parsley, to serve**

Method

1. Sauté the leek and garlic in the oil in a frying pan over low heat until translucent.

2. Add the chopped vegetables and sauté for about 10 more minutes. Transfer to a saucepan or soup pot, add the vegetable stock and bring to the boil. Reduce heat and simmer for about 8 minutes.

3. Blend with a handheld blender or put into a blender.

4. Serve with salt and pepper and top with freshly chopped herbs.

Fish with ginger sauce

SERVES 2

Ingredients

2 fish fillets (white fish is best: perch, ling or barramundi)

1 bunch coriander, chopped

1 red chilli, deseeded, chopped

2 spring onions, chopped

10 roasted almonds, crushed

Ginger sauce

2 tablespoons tamari

1 clove garlic, crushed

1 tablespoon chopped fresh ginger

1 tablespoon chopped lemongrass

½ teaspoon sesame oil

⅓ cup rice vinegar

Method

1. Pan-fry the fish over a medium flame until cooked to your liking.

2. Heat the sauce ingredients in a saucepan over low heat for a few minutes.

3. Remove the fish to a plate and add the sauce over the top.

4. Serve with chopped coriander, chilli and spring onions and sprinkle with the crushed roasted almonds.

Poached chicken and greens

SERVES 2

Ingredients

½ white onion, chopped

1 tablespoon grated fresh ginger

1 clove garlic, crushed

3 cups water

1 chicken breast

2 chicken stock cubes

1 cup chopped zucchini

1 cup chopped broccoli

1 cup chopped spinach

1 bok choy, chopped

Topping sauce

1 tablespoon tamari

2 tablespoons white wine vinegar

1 teaspoon honey

Garnish

¼ cup chopped shallots

¼ cup chopped coriander

salt and pepper

2 tablespoons slivered almonds

Method

1. Add the onion, ginger, garlic and water to a saucepan over medium heat. When the water is simmering, add the chicken and simmer for about 15 minutes or until it is cooked through.

2. Remove the chicken from the pan and set aside. To keep the chicken from drying out, cover it or wrap in some foil.

3. Add the stock cubes to the water, stir, and add the vegetables. Cook for about 10 minutes.

4. Remove the vegetables and place in two bowls. Slice the chicken and place on top. Add a small amount of stock.

5. Mix the topping sauce ingredients and pour over. Top with the garnish ingredients.

Goat cheese and beetroot salad

SERVES 2

Ingredients

2 beetroot

150 grams goat cheese

2 cups chopped rocket

2 tablespoons chopped walnuts

¼ cup chopped coriander

1 spring onion, chopped

Dressing

2 tablespoons olive oil

1 clove garlic, crushed

2 tablespoons red wine vinegar

1 teaspoon honey

salt and pepper, to taste

Method

1. Preheat oven to 180°C. Roughly chop the beetroot and arrange on a baking tray. Bake for 30 minutes, until cooked through. Remove from the oven and cool.

2. Divide the goat cheese, rocket, walnuts, coriander and spring onion into two bowls. Add the beetroot.

3. Put the salad dressing ingredients in a jar and shake to combine. Drizzle over the salad and enjoy.

Bean and halloumi stew

SERVES 3

Ingredients

3 tablespoons olive oil

1 onion, chopped

2 cloves garlic, crushed

1 teaspoon ground coriander

2 tablespoons pesto

1 capsicum, chopped

1 x 425-gram can chopped tomatoes

1 x 400-gram can borlotti beans, drained

200 ml water

150 grams sliced halloumi

½ cup chopped fresh coriander and parsley, to garnish

salt and pepper

Method

1. Heat the oil in a large frying pan, add the onion and garlic and cook until translucent.

2. Add the ground coriander, pesto and capsicum and cook, stirring, for a few minutes. Add the tomatoes and beans and stir through. Add the water, bring to the boil then simmer for about 15 minutes.

3. Heat a frying pan or chargrill pan over medium heat. Add the halloumi and cook until golden brown.

4. Divide the tomato and beans mixture into two bowls. Top with the halloumi and garnish with coriander and parsley. Season to taste.

Salmon one-tray meal

SERVES 1

Ingredients

1 salmon fillet

1 zucchini, thinly sliced

4 yellow scallop squash, thinly sliced

½ cup thinly sliced cauliflower

olive oil, for drizzling

salt and pepper

1 tablespoon chopped parsley

Method

1. Preheat oven to 180°C. Line a baking tray.

2. Place the salmon and vegetables on the baking tray and drizzle with olive oil. Bake for 15–18 minutes.

3. Season to taste and serve topped with parsley.

HEALTH FACT

Salmon is rich in omega-3 fatty acids. The body can't produce these, so we need to include them regularly in our diet. Omega-3 fatty acids contribute to heart health, reduce inflammation, lower blood pressure and can help protect against some cancers, macular degeneration and rheumatoid arthritis. They may also improve memory and protect against Alzheimer's disease and depression.

Detox omelette

SERVES 1

Ingredients

2 eggs

1 teaspoon olive oil

25 grams Danish fetta

¼ cup dill

1 cup chopped spinach

salt and pepper

¼ cup chopped parsley

Method

1. Whisk the eggs. Add oil to a frying pan over medium-high heat. Pour the eggs into the pan and cook for 1–2 minutes, until golden and just set underneath.

2. Place the fetta, dill and spinach on one side of the eggs.

3. Fold one side over. Slide onto a plate and serve topped with freshly chopped parsley.

HEALTH FACT

Dill is loaded with flavonoids that reduce the risk of heart disease. It is very low in calories and strong in flavour so dill is an excellent addition to a healthy detox meal.

Roasted zucchini filled with bean salad

SERVES 2

Ingredients

2 medium-sized zucchini

olive oil

pinch of salt

chopped coriander, to garnish

¼ cup pumpkin seeds, to garnish

Salad filling

¼ cup mixed chopped herbs (parsley, basil and mint)

½ cup white beans, drained and rinsed

⅓ cup halved cherry tomatoes

⅓ cup Danish fetta

I clove garlic, crushed

I lemon, juiced

I tablespoon olive oil

pinch of salt

Optional: I green chilli, sliced

Optional: I red onion, chopped

Method

1. Preheat oven to 180°C. Cut the zucchini lengthwise and remove the seeds and flesh from the inside. Set aside the seeds and flesh. Brush the hollowed-out zucchini with olive oil, sprinkle with salt and bake for 8 minutes.

2. Mix the salad filling ingredients in a bowl. Mix in the seeds and flesh from the zucchini.

3. Remove the zucchini from the oven and spoon the salad ingredients into the centre of each zucchini.

4. Garnish with chopped coriander and pumpkin seeds.

THE
10:10
DIET

THE 600-CALORIE DAYS

THE 600-CALORIE DAYS

The 600-calorie days have been a mainstay in my life for a long time. I love these days – there are loads of health benefits, including lowering blood pressure and cholesterol, anti-aging, strengthening neural connections, increasing human growth hormone, lowering your risk of disease and maintaining a healthy weight.

For maintenance, I do a 600-calorie day every Monday. This sets me up for a good week ahead and corrects any indulgences I have had over the weekend. By indulgence, I mean eating what I please without feeling restricted – that may include bigger portions or something sweet. From a weight-loss perspective, 600-calorie days keep the weight loss in the right direction and are great to ramp up when you are in the dreaded plateau.

People ask me a lot about calorie counting. I only ever count calories on 600-calorie days. My guidelines are:

- 100 calories allowed for beverages, as we still want milk in tea and coffee
- meals are generally around 200 to 250 calories.

Here are some more delicious recipes for your 600-calorie days to keep you on your journey to health and wellness.

Chicken breast and garden salad 255 CALORIES

SERVES 1

Ingredients

1 cos lettuce, leaves separated and torn

5 cherry tomatoes

1 cucumber, sliced

¼ avocado, sliced

1 teaspoon chopped red onion

90 grams cooked skinless chicken breast

Dressing

1 teaspoon olive oil

½ lemon, juiced

salt and pepper

Method

1. Arrange the lettuce and tomatoes on a plate. Top with sliced cucumber, add the avocado slices and sprinkle with chopped red onion.

2. Slice the chicken breast and add to the side of the salad.

3. Combine the dressing ingredients in a jar, shake and pour over the salad.

Smoked salmon and greens 205 CALORIES

SERVES 1

Ingredients

5 asparagus spears

1 cup chopped spinach

1 cup broccoli florets

100 grams smoked salmon

1 teaspoon olive oil

salt and pepper

½ lemon, cut into wedges

Method

1. Lightly steam the vegetables, for about 5 minutes.

2. Place the smoked salmon on a plate and add the steamed vegetables. Drizzle with olive oil. Season to taste and serve with lemon wedges.

 HEALTH FACT *Broccoli really is a superfood. It is low in calories and has a wealth of nutrients making it an excellent choice for skin health, eye health, supporting the immune system, heart health and lowering inflammation.*

Breakfast muffins 90 CALORIES EACH

SERVES 6 (MAKES 12)

Ingredients

1 red capsicum, chopped

12 eggs

¼ cup chopped fresh chives

¾ cup grated cheese

freshly chopped parsley, to serve

salt and pepper

Method

1. Preheat oven to 180°C. Line each cup of a 12-hole muffin tin with baking paper unless using a silicone muffin tray.

2. Divide the capsicum evenly among each muffin hole.

3. Beat the eggs well in a large bowl. Add the chopped chives. Pour the egg mixture into the muffin holes. Add a teaspoon of cheese to each muffin hole.

4. Bake for 12–15 minutes, until golden brown and cooked through.

5. Serve with chopped fresh parsley and salt and pepper.

Chicken pho 298 CALORIES

SERVES 2

Ingredients

2 teaspoons coriander seeds

I clove

2 spring onions, chopped

I litre chicken broth

200 grams skinless chicken breast

2 cups water

pinch of salt

I teaspoon maple syrup

3 teaspoons fish sauce

pepper

½ lime, cut into wedges

I red chilli, chopped

I bunch coriander

Method

1. Add the coriander seeds, clove and spring onion to a soup pot.

2. Pour in the chicken broth. Add chicken breast, water and salt. Bring to the boil and simmer for about 10 minutes, or until the chicken breast is cooked through. Remove the chicken breast and shred.

3. Cook the broth for a further 10 minutes to reduce. Now strain the broth. Add maple syrup and fish sauce to the broth. Season with pepper to taste.

4. Serve with lime wedges, freshly chopped red chilli and coriander leaves.

Simple egg salad 200 CALORIES

SERVES 2

Ingredients

2 eggs

1 tomato, chopped

1 cucumber, sliced

1 cup chopped iceberg lettuce

Dressing

1 teaspoon olive oil

squeeze of lemon juice

salt and pepper, to taste

1 teaspoon chopped parsley

Method

1. Drop the eggs in boiling water for 8 minutes. Remove and cool under running cold water.

2. Put the tomato, cucumber and lettuce in a bowl, slice the egg over the top.

3. Mix the dressing ingredients, pour over the salad, and enjoy.

Chicken meatballs and green salad 260 CALORIES

SERVES 2

Ingredients

250 grams chicken mince

I egg

15 grams almond meal

I tablespoon freshly chopped parsley

2 teaspoons olive oil

Green salad

I cup chopped rocket

I tablespoon diced red onion

squeeze of lemon juice

salt and pepper

Method

1. Mix chicken mince, egg, almond meal and parsley and shape into six meatballs.

2. Add the oil to a frying pan and cook the chicken meatballs over medium heat until browned.

3. Toss the rocket with onion, lemon juice, salt and pepper. Serve with the chicken.

Naked burger 160 CALORIES

SERVES 1

Ingredients

100 grams chicken mince

½ teaspoon olive oil

1 slice cheese

1 slice tomato

2 iceberg lettuce leaves

1 slice onion

Method

1. Shape chicken mince into a patty. Cook with olive oil in a frying pan over medium heat until browned.

2. Assemble the ingredients as you would a burger. Place the chicken patty on a plate and top with cheese, tomato, lettuce and onion. Enjoy.

HEALTH FACT

Chicken is a white protein that has great nutritional value and is low in saturated fat. It has high amounts of omega-6 fatty acids, and minerals, such as vitamin B6, which is important for circulation and brain health, may help reduce morning sickness and helps improve your mood.

Tuna, greens and chilli 152 CALORIES

SERVES 1

Ingredients

½ **cup chopped cauliflower**

½ **cup broccoli florets**

½ **zucchini, sliced**

1 x 95-gram can tuna, drained

1 birdseye chilli, deseeded, chopped

squeeze of lemon juice

salt and pepper

½ **teaspoon olive oil**

Method

1. Steam the cauliflower, broccoli and zucchini for a few minutes.

2. Place the tuna on a plate and add the steamed vegetables. Top with chopped chilli.

3. Add lemon juice, salt and pepper and a drizzle of olive oil.

Low-cal cauliflower soup 260 CALORIES

SERVES 2

Ingredients

2 tablespoons olive oil

½ onion, chopped

2 cloves garlic, chopped

½ head cauliflower

3 cups chicken stock

50 ml almond milk

salt and pepper, to taste

fresh thyme, to serve

Method

1. Add the olive oil, onion and garlic to a saucepan and cook over low heat until translucent.

2. Add the cauliflower and chicken stock. Increase heat to medium and cook for about 20 minutes.

3. Add the milk, salt and pepper. Blitz with a handheld blender until smooth, or transfer to a regular blender.

4. Sprinkle with fresh thyme and serve.

Garlic prawn salad 193 CALORIES

SERVES 1

Ingredients

6 cooked, peeled prawns

½ cup peas

5 asparagus spears

1 teaspoon oil

¼ cup chopped coriander, to serve

**1 teaspoon fresh cayenne chilli,
to serve**

Marinade

1 clove garlic, crushed

2 teaspoons chopped fresh ginger

1 chilli, deseeded, chopped

1 teaspoon olive oil

¼ cup freshly chopped parsley

Method

1. Mix the prawns with the marinade in a glass bowl. Cover and set aside for a minimum of 15 minutes. You can leave in the refrigerator for a few hours if you like.

2. Pan-fry the prawns, peas and asparagus in oil over medium heat for 3–4 minutes, or until cooked to your liking.

3. Serve with the freshly chopped coriander and chilli. Delish.

Tofu stir-fry 216 CALORIES

SERVES 1

Ingredients

1 tablespoon sesame oil

150 grams firm tofu, diced

1 tablespoon tamari

1 clove garlic, crushed

1 spring onion, chopped

1 tablespoon grated fresh ginger

1 handful spinach leaves

1 tablespoon sesame seeds, to serve

Method

1. Heat sesame oil in a frying pan over medium heat. Add the diced tofu. Add tamari, garlic, onion and ginger and toss around the pan for a few minutes.

2. Add the spinach leaves and allow to wilt briefly.

3. Serve with a sprinkle of sesame seeds and enjoy.

HEALTH FACT

Compounds in sesame seeds can help get rid of the bacteria in your mouth that causes plaque on your teeth. This antibacterial property can also help fight common skin infections, such as athlete's foot.

Niçoise salad 280 CALORIES

SERVES 1

Ingredients

80 grams cooked tuna

1 hard-boiled egg

8 Sicilian or Kalamata olives

handful romaine lettuce

½ cucumber, chopped

5 cherry tomatoes, halved

¼ red onion, finely diced

2 green beans, chopped

1 teaspoon olive oil

squeeze of lemon juice

salt and pepper

Method

1. Combine tuna, egg, olives and salad vegetables in a bowl.

2. Drizzle with olive oil and lemon juice and season to taste.

Note: a small 95-gram tin of tuna can be used instead of fresh tuna.

Oven-baked chilli barramundi 186 CALORIES

SERVES I

Ingredients

100 grams barramundi

I clove garlic, chopped

I tablespoon grated fresh ginger

I birdseye chilli, deseeded, chopped

I spring onion, chopped

I zucchini, chopped

I cup broccoli florets

salt and pepper

squeeze of lemon

I small handful coriander

Method

1. Preheat oven to 190°C. Wrap the fish in foil with the garlic, ginger, chilli and onion. Bake for 12–15 minutes.

2. Steam the zucchini and broccoli until just tender.

3. Place the fish and vegetables on a plate. Season to taste, squeeze over lemon juice and garnish with coriander.

HEALTH FACT

Barramundi is low in fat. It has half the fat of other fish, such as salmon, but is still packed with omega-3 fatty acids, which are known to promote both brain and cardiovascular health.

Greek-style omelette wrap 189 CALORIES

SERVES 1

Ingredients

1 egg

½ teaspoon olive oil

1 teaspoon chopped dill

½ cup spinach leaves

40 grams fetta, grated

salt and pepper

Method

1. Whisk the egg in a bowl. Add olive oil to a frying pan over medium-high heat. Pour the beaten egg into the pan and swish it around to look like a pancake. Flip it over to cook the other side and remove to a plate.

2. Add the dill, spinach and fetta to the omelette, season to taste, and roll it up like a wrap. Cut in half and enjoy.

Turkey roll-up 181 CALORIES

SERVES 1

Ingredients

100 grams sliced turkey breast

1 spring onion, chopped

¼ red capsicum, sliced

1 teaspoon good-quality mayonnaise

salt and pepper

1 leaf butter lettuce

Method

Assemble the ingredients down the centre of the lettuce leaf. Roll up tightly and cut in half.

HEALTH FACT *Turkey is a great source of protein. The body needs protein to help build and repair bones, muscles, skin, cartilage and blood. Your body can't store protein, so it is important to eat it every day. Turkey is also rich in tryptophan, which can improve sleep, relieve depression and anxiety, and help lift your mood.*

One-tray
fish and capsicum 290 CALORIES

SERVES 1

Ingredients

120 grams perch

1 capsicum, sliced

1 teaspoon olive oil

salt and pepper

2 sprigs thyme

6 olives (I use Sicilian)

1 handful parsley leaves

Dressing

1 teaspoon olive oil

1 teaspoon balsamic vinegar

1 clove garlic, crushed

Method

1. Preheat oven to 190°C. Line a baking tray.

2. Place the fish in the centre and place the sliced capsicum around it. Drizzle with olive oil and season with salt and pepper. Sprinkle with thyme. Bake for 15 minutes.

3. Mix the dressing ingredients in a bowl or jar.

4. Place the fish and capsicum on a plate and add the dressing. Add the olives and parsley.

Beetroot, cottage cheese and lentil salad 176 CALORIES

SERVES 1

Ingredients

1 beetroot

1 cup chopped spinach

¼ cup cooked lentils

1 tablespoon chopped red onion

¼ cup chopped chives and parsley

1 tablespoon cottage cheese

salt and pepper

Dressing

1 clove garlic, crushed

1 teaspoon apple cider vinegar

1 teaspoon olive oil

½ teaspoon honey

½ teaspoon Dijon mustard

Method

1. Preheat oven to 180°C. Chop the beetroot and arrange on a baking tray. Bake for 30 minutes. Remove and let cool.

2. Add the dressing ingredients to a bowl or jar and mix well.

3. Place the spinach and lentils on a plate, add the beetroot, onion and fresh herbs.

4. Pour on the dressing, top with cottage cheese and season to taste.

Fetta and broccolini one-tray meal 203 CALORIES

SERVES 1

Ingredients

1 bunch broccolini

5 cherry tomatoes

¼ chopped red onion, chopped

50 grams Danish fetta

1 lemon, cut into wedges

1 teaspoon olive oil

¼ teaspoon chilli flakes

1 handful fresh parsley, chopped, to garnish

salt and pepper

Method

1. Preheat oven to 190°C. Line a baking tray.

2. Assemble the broccolini, tomatoes, onion, fetta and lemon wedges on the baking tray. Drizzle with the olive oil and sprinkle with chilli flakes. Bake for 20 minutes.

3. Garnish with parsley and season to taste.

Capsicum and eggs 200 CALORIES

SERVES 1

Ingredients

½ **capsicum**

1 **teaspoon olive oil**

2 **eggs**

1 **tablespoon chopped chives**

salt and pepper

Method

1. Preheat oven to 180°C. Cut a capsicum crossways to make 2 rings. Heat olive oil in an oven-proof frying pan. Place the rings in the pan and cook for 2 minutes.

2. Flip the capsicum rings over. Break an egg into each of the capsicum rings.

3. Place the frying pan in the oven for 6–8 minutes, or until the eggs are cooked.

4. Serve with chopped chives, salt and pepper.

Spicy silken tofu 214 CALORIES

SERVES 2

Ingredients

250 grams silken tofu

2 tablespoons coriander

1 tablespoon chopped spring onion

2 teaspoons white sesame seeds

Spicy dressing

½ tablespoon sesame oil

1 teaspoon dried chilli

2 tablespoons tamari

1 teaspoon honey

Method

1. Combine the spicy dressing ingredients in a bowl or jar.

2. Remove the silken tofu from the packet and drain. Put in a bowl and pour the dressing over the top.

3. Add the coriander, spring onion and sesame seeds.

White beans and herbs 240 CALORIES

SERVES 1

Ingredients

1 teaspoon olive oil

1 clove garlic, crushed

½ cup cooked white beans

¼ cup chicken stock

salt and pepper

½ cup chopped spinach, to serve

½ cup chopped rocket, to serve

Herb oil

1 teaspoon olive oil

2 tablespoons lemon juice

¼ cup chopped chives

¼ cup chopped basil leaves

salt and pepper

Method

1. Heat the olive oil in a small saucepan. Add the garlic, beans and chicken stock and cook for about 5 minutes.

2. To prepare the herb oil, blitz the ingredients in a blender.

3. Add the beans to a bowl and swirl the herb oil on top, then season to taste. Serve with the spinach and rocket.

SMOOTHIES

SMOOTHIES

There is a wonderful proverb that necessity is the mother of invention and this applies to my love and journey with smoothies.

I find smoothies so effective when you are time poor, but they are also a great way to enjoy a range of ingredients for health benefits that you wouldn't think would go well together but work in a smoothie.

With smoothies, you also get all the benefits of fruit and vegetables as well as enjoying the peel. I am a big believer in eating the peel of all fruit and vegetables – this is where we can get so much insoluble fibre that is good for gut health, lowering risk of heart disease and supporting healthy hormonal clearance. There is a plethora of research that shows just how important fibre is for long-term health and wellness, and a smoothie is the perfect solution to add more fibre to your diet.

Plus, they keep you full longer and taste sensational with their creamy texture. It can almost feel like a dessert.

My basic rule for a smoothie is make sure there is always a protein in there to keep you full and give you that slow release of energy throughout your morning. Here are some of my favourites to add:

- chia
- yoghurt
- nuts
- nut butter
- protein powder.

Of course, vegetables and fruit are a given. My tip to make the smoothie extra delicious it to use only ripe fruit, as fruit is sweeter when ripe. That way, you can avoid adding any sweetener, but if you do have a sweet tooth like me, a teaspoon of raw honey will not break your diet. After all, it needs to taste good, too.

All the recipes I create, I do so with a purpose, so you will see the titles of my smoothies showing the intention of their creation. These also align with my holistic approach to health, wellness and healthy weight loss.

All you need to make smoothies is a good kitchen appliance to blitz. For each smoothie, place all the ingredients into the blender, blitz and serve. All recipes are for I serving size.

When making smoothies, my recommendation for milk is only to use almond milk, primarily because it is the lowest in calories, but it also contains vitamins A, D and E, so using it boosts your body's immune system. It is rich in vitamin B and iron which both increase muscle strength and healing.

Note: you can interchange Greek yoghurt and protein powder in these smoothies. The protein powder needs to be no more than 100 calories.

Sarah's wellness smoothie

1 tablespoon grated fresh ginger
1 kiwi fruit, chopped
1 teaspoon nut butter
1 cup chopped spinach
¼ avocado
½ green apple
1 teaspoon raw honey
½ cup water
2 tablespoons Greek yoghurt
  or protein powder
4 ice cubes

Sarah's debloating smoothie

1 tablespoon Greek yoghurt
or protein powder
½ cup frozen pineapple pieces
½ cup water
¼ cup chopped fresh mint
2 teaspoons grated fresh ginger
½ frozen banana
1 teaspoon chia seeds
4–5 ice cubes

Anti-Inflammatory smoothie

½ cup frozen pineapple
½ cup berries
1 teaspoon ginger
½ teaspoon turmeric
1 teaspoon honey
10 cashews
1 tablespoon Greek yoghurt
½ cup chopped kale
1 teaspoon olive oil
½ cup water
4 ice cubes

Gut-friendly smoothie

½ cup frozen raspberries
½ cup water
2 tablespoons Greek yoghurt
½ apple (with skin on)
I teaspoon almond butter
½ teaspoon cinnamon
I tablespoon chia seeds
I teaspoon flax meal
 4 ice cubes

Memory-building smoothie

½ cup frozen blueberries
I cup chopped spinach
2 teaspoons cacao
10 almonds
¼ avocado
½ cup almond milk or water
I scoop protein powder
4–5 ice cubes

Immunity-building smoothie

I tablespoon fresh ginger
I tablespoon Greek yoghurt
I cup chopped spinach
I kiwi fruit, chopped
⅓ cup chopped pineapple
¼ cup blueberries
I teaspoon raw honey
½ cup water
4 ice cubes

Energy-lifting smoothie

½ apple (with skin on)
½ cup water
¼ avocado
I tablespoon Greek yoghurt
½ cup strawberries

½ cup spinach
I teaspoon nut butter
I teaspoon chia seeds
5 ice cubes

Stress-less smoothie

2 brazil nuts
I teaspoon chia seeds
I kiwi fruit, chopped
½ cup blueberries
½ cup chopped spinach
I teaspoon matcha powder
2 tablespoons Greek yoghurt
  or protein powder
½ cup water
4 ice cubes

Antioxidant-rich smoothie

½ cup chopped kale
I cup frozen blueberries
½ cup Greek yoghurt
  or protein powder
⅓ cup water
½ teaspoon ground cinnamon
I teaspoon almond butter
3 pecans
4–6 ice cubes

Anti-aging smoothie

½ cup guava
I cup chopped kale
¼ cup blueberries
¼ cup strawberries
5 cashew
I tablespoon chia seeds
½ cup water
I scoop protein powder
½ teaspoon cinnamon
5 ice cubes

VEGAN AND VEGETARIAN OPTIONS

VEGAN AND VEGETARIAN OPTIONS

I have always loved vegan and vegetarian dishes. Many of my meals throughout the week are meat-free.

In my years of planning diets for people, I have seen a lot of people fall into an increase in carbohydrates and fats when taking on vegan and vegetarian diets.

Making sure you have enough protein is really important for growth, development and weight-loss satiety.

I am going to share with you some vegan and vegetarian meals that are healthy and absolutely delicious.

Roasted pumpkin and goat cheese

SERVES 4

Ingredients

½ **medium pumpkin, cut into thick wedges**

2 **tablespoons olive oil**

salt and pepper

pinch of cinnamon

1 **tablespoon chopped fresh sage**

150 **grams goat cheese**

¼ **cup pumpkin seeds**

Method

1. Preheat oven to 180°C. Arrange the pumpkin on a baking tray with the olive oil, salt, pepper, cinnamon and sage. Bake for 30 minutes, turning at 15 minutes.

2. Once the pumpkin is cooked, add to a plate and serve with goat cheese and pumpkin seeds.

Pumpkin is low in calories. One cup has only 49 calories. Pumpkin is a great source of beta-carotene, which your body converts into vitamin A. Vitamin A strengthens your immune system and helps fight infections. Just one cup of pumpkin gives you 245 per cent of your recommended daily value of vitamin A.

Black bean patties

SERVES 2

Ingredients

1 x 445-gram can black beans, drained

3 cloves garlic, finely chopped

½ onion, finely chopped

½ capsicum, finely chopped

1 egg

½ cup almond meal

yoghurt, olive oil, chilli flakes, fresh herbs, salt and pepper, to serve

Method

1. Preheat oven to 180°C. Mash the beans with a fork until thick and pasty. Add the chopped garlic, onion and capsicum to the beans.

2. Add the egg and almond meal to the mix and divide into 4 patties.

3. Place the patties on a baking tray and bake for 20 minutes, turning at the halfway point.

4. Serve with a dollop of yoghurt, a drizzle of olive oil, a sprinkle of chilli flakes, chopped fresh herbs, and salt and pepper.

Ricotta and zucchini cannelloni

SERVES 6

Ingredients

6 zucchini

I egg

½ cup grated parmesan cheese

¼ cup fresh spinach

2 tablespoons chopped fresh basil

salt and pepper

I ½ cups ricotta

2 cups passata

Topping

I tablespoon olive oil

¾ cup mozzarella cheese

salt and pepper

I tablespoon grated parmesan cheese

I handful fresh basil

Method

1. Preheat oven to 180°C. Using a potato peeler, slice the zucchini into strips. You should have about 25–30 strips.

2. Add the egg, parmesan, spinach, basil, salt, pepper and ricotta to a bowl and mix well.

3. Add the passata to a baking dish.

4. Place the ricotta mixture at the start of a zucchini strip and roll. Then place in the baking dish on the pasta sauce. Repeat until each zucchini strip is filled. Stack tightly as you add them to the baking dish.

5. Top with olive oil, mozzarella, salt and pepper and a touch more parmesan.

6. Bake for about 30 minutes and serve with fresh basil.

Egg salad lettuce wrap

SERVES 1

Ingredients

2 eggs

¼ tomato, sliced

1 teaspoon chopped white onion

3 slices beetroot

1 large lettuce leaf

salt and pepper

Method

1. Drop the eggs in boiling water for 8 minutes. Remove and cool under running cold water.

2. Place the sliced tomato, onion and beetroot down the centre of the lettuce leaf. Slice the eggs and add. Season to taste. Roll up and enjoy.

HEALTH FACT

Lettuce is a terrific source of vitamin K, which can help reduce the risk of developing cataracts and can help strengthen bones. A lettuce is also great for hydration as more than 95 per cent of a raw lettuce is made up of water.

Ratatouille

SERVES 4

Ingredients

2 tablespoons olive oil

1 onion, chopped

4 cloves garlic, crushed

2 zucchini, chopped

1 eggplant, chopped

1 capsicum, chopped

2 cups chopped cherry tomatoes

salt and pepper

fresh parsley and basil

Method

1. Heat oil in a saucepan over low heat. Add the onion and garlic and cook until transparent.

2. Add the chopped vegetables and cook for 30 minutes. Season to taste.

3. Serve with the freshly chopped parsley and basil.

HEALTH FACT

Eggplant is a high-fibre, low-calorie food that is packed with nutrients and has many health benefits. One cup of eggplant has only 20 calories, so is excellent for weight loss. They are rich in anthocyanins, which are antioxidants known to protect cells against free-radical damage. Eggplant is also excellent for heart health.

Tofu scramble – the vegan breakfast alternative

SERVES 1

Ingredients

120 grams firm tofu

1 teaspoon olive oil

¼ teaspoon turmeric powder

sea salt and freshly ground pepper

**freshly chopped chives and
 parsley, to serve**

Method

1. Using a fork, crumble the tofu to small pieces.

2. Heat olive oil in a frying pan over low heat, add the tofu and turmeric and cook, stirring, for 5 minutes. Season to taste.

3. Serve with freshly chopped chives and parsley.

 HEALTH FACT

Tofu is made from soybean curd and contains isoflavones, which are powerful antioxidants. It is also rich in iron and calcium. Eat it to alleviate menopausal symptoms, reduce cholesterol, reduce your risk of diabetes and help reduce the risk of some cancers.

Spicy mushrooms

SERVES 2

Ingredients

2 tablespoons oil

2 cups mushrooms, stems removed

2 cloves garlic, crushed

1 spring onion, finely chopped

1 tablespoon grated fresh ginger

1 tablespoon chopped fresh mint

squeeze of lime juice

salt and pepper

1 green cayenne pepper

2 tablespoons roasted almonds

Method

1. Heat the oil in a frying pan. Add the mushrooms and cook for about 5 minutes. Add garlic, spring onion and ginger. Stir for another few minutes.

2. Add the mint, lime juice, salt, pepper, green cayenne pepper and almonds. Toss and serve.

 HEALTH FACT

Ginger is one of the healthiest spices you can eat. It is well known for its anti-nausea properties and can help treat morning sickness, sea sickness, nausea from chemotherapy as well as nausea from surgery. Ginger can also reduce blood sugar levels, lower cholesterol, help osteoarthritis and fight infections.

Tomato, fetta and mint salad

SERVES 1

Ingredients

5 roma tomatoes, chopped

½ red onion, finely chopped

1 handful mint leaves

1 tablespoon olive oil

1 tablespoon balsamic vinegar

salt and pepper

50 grams Danish fetta, cubed

Method

1   Add the chopped tomatoes, onion and mint to a bowl.

2.   Add olive oil and balsamic vinegar. Season to taste.

3.   Top with the Danish fetta cubes.

HEALTH FACT

Mint may help alleviate the symptoms of irritable bowel syndrome, such as stomach pain, gas and bloating. It may also help relieve indigestion. Research also shows that mint can help with bad breath, improve cold symptoms by getting rid of nasal congestion and improve energy levels. Mint can also help reduce menstrual cramps.

Avocado and egg salad

SERVES 2

Ingredients

4 eggs

I avocado

I teaspoon Dijon mustard

I lemon, juiced

I clove garlic, finely chopped

½ red onion, chopped

I cup chopped rocket

½ capsicum, chopped

6 Sicilian olives (or use any green olives)

I tablespoon chia seeds

salt and pepper

Method

1. Drop the eggs in boiling water for 8 minutes. Remove and cool under running cold water.

2. Mash the avocado with mustard, lemon juice and garlic. Slice the eggs.

3. Combine the avocado with onion, rocket, capsicum and olives in a bowl. Top with sliced egg and sprinkle with chia seeds. Season to taste.

 HEALTH FACT *Red onions contain sulfur compounds that protect the body from ulcers and fight bacteria in the urinary tract. It's best to eat them raw as cooking can reduce their health benefits.*

Fibre-rich vegan salad

SERVES 2

Ingredients

1 onion, chopped

1 capsicum, chopped

1 carrot, grated

1 cup white beans

½ cup corn kernels

1 cup chopped spinach

1 cup chopped rocket

Dressing

1 clove garlic, crushed

1 lemon, juiced

1 tablespoon olive oil

1 teaspoon Dijon mustard

1 teaspoon honey

salt and pepper, to taste

Topping

15 shelled pistachios

¼ cup chopped coriander leaves

Method

1. Combine the salad ingredients in a bowl.

2. Put the dressing ingredients in a jar and shake well.

3. Add the dressing to the salad and top with the pistachios and coriander.

SNACKS

SNACKS

I am a big believer in the importance of snacks. They keep you going between meals and can really take away that feeling of being famished and ravenous, which generally means you won't overeat at meals.

My basic guidelines for snacks are that they need to contain protein as that really does help you keep full, which is the objective of a snack. This protein can be plant- or animal-based.

I am going to share with you some of my favourite snacks to continue to enjoy on the 10:10 Diet journey, as well as a couple for maintenance that are sensational.

Cherry tomatoes with mozzarella cheese

Pear and ricotta cheese

Cinnamon and flaxseed

Cucumber and hummus

Ricotta and cacao

10:10 Diet snacks

A piece of fruit, such as:
1 apple, mandarin, orange or pear, or
1 cup berries

½ a protein bar at 100 calories

Nuts and berries
8 almonds
¼ cup strawberries

Mixed nuts
15 nuts:
5 almonds
5 cashews
5 pistachios

Yoghurt, dill and celery
3 stalks celery
1 tablespoon yoghurt
½ teaspoon dill
(mixed into the yoghurt)

Tuna and capsicum
½ capsicum, cut at the cross section
40 grams tuna (simply use ½ a 95-gram
can of tuna)

Cucumber and hummus
1 cup cucumber
50 grams hummus

Cherry tomatoes with mozzarella cheese
½ cup cherry tomatoes
30 grams mozzarella cheese

Pear and ricotta cheese
½ pear, sliced
50 grams ricotta

Ricotta and cacao
¼ cup ricotta
½ teaspoon cacao
pinch of stevia

Cinnamon and flaxseed
¼ cup cottage cheese
2 teaspoons ground flaxseeds
¼ teaspoon cinnamon
pinch of stevia

Kale chips
Ingredients
1 cup chopped kale leaves
1 tablespoon olive oil
pinch of salt

Method

Preheat oven to 180°C. Line a baking tray.
Mix the kale in the olive oil and salt.
Lay on the tray and bake for about 10 minutes
but check so they don't burn.

Protein balls

MAKES 14. SERVING SIZE 1

Ingredients

10 Medjool dates, pitted

½ cup shredded coconut

1 scoop protein powder (chocolate or vanilla flavoured)

⅓ cup almond butter (peanut butter is also fine)

2 teaspoons cinnamon

2 teaspoons vanilla extract

Method

1. Add all the ingredients to the food processor and blitz until well combined.

2. Roll a tablespoon of the mixture in the palm of your hand into a ball.

3. Store in the refrigerator. Easy and delicious.

HEALTH FACT

Dates are full of fibre making them excellent for your digestive health by preventing constipation. The fibre in dates is also great for helping to control blood sugar levels. They are high in disease-fighting antioxidants as well as being an excellent natural sweetener.

Sarah's matcha bars

MAKES 10. SERVING SIZE 1

Ingredients

⅓ cup cocoa powder

1 cup almonds

2 tablespoons matcha powder,
  plus extra to decorate

2 tablespoons coconut oil

½ cup coconut flakes

½ cup maple syrup

2 cups pitted dates

Method

1. Combine all ingredients in a food processor and blitz. (If your dough is clumpy, continue to blitz until well combined. It only takes a few minutes.)

2. Line a baking tray and spread the mixture on the tray. Press it into the shape of a rectangle about 2.5 cm thick and refrigerate for a few hours.

3. Cut into your desired shapes using a cookie cutter or simply cut into neat rectangles.

4. For final decoration, sprinkle with matcha powder to serve. So healthy and absolutely delicious.

Sarah's immunity-boosting slice

MAKES 12. SERVING SIZE 1

Base

2 cups rolled oats

1 cup desiccated coconut

**1 cup Medjool dates or
pitted dates, soaked**

1 ½ tablespoons grated fresh ginger

**1 tablespoon fresh or
powdered turmeric**

1 tablespoon coconut oil

1 tablespoon vanilla extract

pinch of salt

⅓ cup maple syrup

Icing

1 cup desiccated coconut

1 cup cashews

½ cup tahini

½ cup sesame seeds

1 tablespoon grated fresh ginger

½ lemon, juiced

½ cup coconut oil

pinch of salt

⅓ cup maple syrup

1 tablespoon peanut butter

Method

1. Put all the base ingredients into a food processor or blender and blend well. Press into a lined baking dish and put in the freezer.

2. Place all the icing ingredients into a food processor. Blend well for a few minutes, until creamy.

3. Remove the base from the freezer and spread the icing over the top. Freeze again, preferably overnight for best results. Slice and enjoy.

GUILT-FREE
DESSERTS

GUILT-FREE DESSERTS

A part of learning to maintain your new healthy weight is learning to enjoy all foods, including desserts. One thing I want for my community is for people to love and appreciate food.

Most of the people I have met love a good dessert, but they have always been considered taboo, leaving you feeling guilty if you eat one. Mainstream desserts are generally full of refined sugar, and this does lead to weight gain.

I love a good dessert and have a sweet tooth, so I started to experiment with creating delicious desserts that are guilt-free and even have health benefits. Life is too short not to enjoy the foods you love but portion control is key.

Here are my favourite guilt-free desserts. You will never look back once you have tried these. Just remember that a serving size of a dessert should be around the size of your palm or 80 grams.

Sarah's chia tiramisu

SERVES 4

Ingredients

6 tablespoons white chia seeds

375 ml almond milk

1 tablespoon coconut sugar

4 tablespoons maple syrup

pinch of salt

½ lemon, juiced

1 teaspoon vanilla extract

3 tablespoons cocoa powder

1 teaspoon instant coffee

Toppings

4 tablespoons coconut yoghurt, to layer

fine instant coffee, to dust over

dark chocolate shavings, to garnish

Method

1. You will need 8 glasses or glass cups.

2. Divide chia seeds, almond milk, coconut sugar, maple syrup and salt evenly among 4 glasses or glass cups. Stir each one to combine.

3. Fill the glasses as follows:
   Add to the first glass: lemon juice and ½ teaspoon vanilla extract.
   Add to the second glass: 1 tablespoon cocoa powder.
   Add to the third glass: ½ tablespoon cocoa powder and 1 teaspoon instant coffee.
   Add to the fourth glass: 1½ tablespoons cocoa powder and ½ teaspoon vanilla extract.

4. Stir each glass to mix well and refrigerate overnight.

5. To assemble – the fun part – simply spoon some chia mixture from the fourth glass (cocoa and vanilla) into the bottom of a new glass, then add a tablespoon of coconut yoghurt. Add some chia mixture from the third glass (cocoa and coffee), then add a tablespoon of coconut yoghurt. Add some chia mixture from the second glass (cocoa powder), then add a tablespoon of coconut yoghurt. Finally, add some chia mixture from the first glass (lemon juice and vanilla extract) to the top and finish with a tablespoon of coconut yoghurt. Repeat for the other 3 glasses.

6. Dust the top of the mixture in each glass with coffee and arrange chocolate shards on top.

Tofu brownies

SERVES 8

Ingredients

¾ cup silken tofu

½ cup water

2 tablespoons coconut oil

½ cup maple syrup

2 teaspoons vanilla extract

1¾ cups oat flour

1 teaspoon baking powder

2 tablespoons stevia

½ cup cocoa

pinch of salt

Method

1. Preheat oven to 180°C. Combine the tofu, water, coconut oil, maple syrup and vanilla extract in a bowl and stir until smooth.

2. In another bowl, mix the flour, baking powder, stevia, cocoa and salt.

3. Combine the wet and dry ingredients.

4. Line a baking pan or lightly spray it with olive oil. Bake the brownies for 30 minutes.

Fruit dip

SERVES 4

Ingredients

3 tablespoons smooth peanut butter

2 tablespoons raw honey

2 cups Greek yoghurt

Fruit for dipping

apples

bananas

grapes

pears

strawberries

Method

1. Make sure the peanut butter and honey are at room temperature. Blend until well combined.

2. Add the yoghurt and whisk until smooth.

3. Slice the fruit and serve immediately.

Sarah's cottage cheese mousse

SERVES 4 – 6

Ingredients

500 grams cottage cheese

3 tablespoons cocoa

2 scoops protein powder

2 tablespoons stevia

Method

1. Place everything in a food processor and blitz until it is a mousse-like consistency.

2. Put into little serving dishes or in one glass dish and chill immediately. So easy!

Sarah's healthy chocolate avocado mousse

SERVES 6

Ingredients

2 ripe medium-sized avocados

½ cup cacao

½ cup melted dark chocolate chips

3 tablespoons almond milk

1 teaspoon vanilla extract

pinch of salt

⅓ cup maple syrup

5 Medjool dates, pitted

Method

Combine all ingredients in a blender or food processor and blend until completely smooth. Refrigerate for at least an hour.

Cacoa is underestimated for all its amazing health benefits. It has the highest plant-based source of iron, is rich in magnesium and potassium, has more calcium than cows' milk and is one of the best sources of antioxidants. It can help lower blood pressure, reduce the symptoms of irritable bowel syndrome, reduce the risk of diabetes and reduce inflammation.

Sarah's healthy mini cheesecakes with chia berry compote

SERVES 6

Crust

1 cup cashews

1 cup pitted dates

tiny pinch of salt

Cheesecake filling

250 grams cream cheese

1 cup good-quality Greek yoghurt

⅓ cup honey

1 tablespoon lemon juice

1 tablespoon vanilla extract

tiny pinch of salt

Chia berry compote

2 cups mixed berries (strawberries, blueberries, blackberries)

2 tablespoons chia seeds

2 tablespoons honey

½ lemon, juiced

Method

1. To make the crust, simply add the cashews, dates and salt to a food processor and blitz until blended.

2. In a 6-hole muffin tray, line the muffin cups with baking paper, unless using a silicone muffin tray. Add about a tablespoon of the mix to the base of each muffin cup.

3. For the cheesecake filling, place all filling ingredients in a food processor or blender and blitz until smooth. Spoon this mixture in to the muffin cups. Refrigerate for a few hours before serving.

4. For the compote, cook the berries in a saucepan over low heat for 5 minutes. Add the chia seeds, honey, and lemon juice to the saucepan. Cook for a further 5 minutes. Place the compote in a jar and refrigerate. If you have any compote left over, use it as a delicious jam.

5. To serve, remove the cheesecakes from the muffin cups and simply add the chia compote to the cheesecakes. Delicious.

Sarah's blueberry and banana ice cream

SERVES 6

Ingredients

3 frozen bananas

2 cups frozen blueberries

2 tablespoons nut butter

2 teaspoons vanilla essence

Method

Simply blitz in a blender, scoop into a container and freeze. Super healthy, guilt free and next-level delicious!

HEALTH FACT

Bananas are an excellent source of potassium, which is important for lowering blood pressure and protecting against heart disease. They are also high in pectin, a soluble fibre that helps lower cholesterol and maintain good bowel function. Bananas are also a great energy booster and can help improve your mood.

Chocolate, nut butter and date treats

MAKES 20. SERVING SIZE 2

Ingredients

20 Medjool dates, pitted

⅓ cup nut butter

250 grams dark chocolate

½ cup crushed roasted almonds

Method

1. Line a baking tray. Cut each date down the centre but only to create a gap so you can fill each date with ½ a teaspoon of nut butter. Place the filled dates on the tray and put them in the refrigerator for 30 minutes.

2. Meanwhile, melt the chocolate in a glass bowl over a saucepan of boiling water

3. Once melted, roll each date through the chocolate and place back on the baking paper.

4. Sprinkle them with the crushed roasted almonds. Return to the refrigerator for a further 30 minutes. Once done, you can keep these in the refrigerator for an easy snack and some energy on the go that is guilt free and completely delicious, or save for a sweet treat as a dessert.

Sarah's cute chocolate bites

MAKES 20. SERVING SIZE 2

Ingredients

1½ cups roasted almonds

⅓ cup nut butter (you can use peanut butter)

2 tablespoons maple syrup

1–2 drops vanilla essence

1 cup dark chocolate

Method

1. Blitz the almonds in a food processor. Add the nut butter, maple syrup and vanilla essence and blitz until well combined. Line a slice pan or dish. Press the mixture into the dish and freeze for 45 minutes.

2. Remove from the freezer and cut into cute squares about 3 cm square.

3. Melt the chocolate in a glass bowl over a saucepan of boiling water. Dip the squares in the melted chocolate and set aside on a large plate so the squares aren't touching. Let them set for an hour in the refrigerator.

Maple syrup is an excellent natural sweetener. It contains a molecule called quebecol, which has anti-inflammatory properties that have been shown to decrease the risk of many diseases and cancers.

Sarah's avocado, banana and dark chocolate ice cream

SERVES 2

Ingredients

2 frozen bananas

1 avocado

1 tablespoon peanut butter

1 teaspoon vanilla paste

1 teaspoon vanilla essence

¼ cup maple syrup

3 tablespoons cacao powder

¼ cup dark chocolate chips

Method

1. Place the frozen bananas in a food processor along with the avocado, peanut butter, vanilla paste, vanilla essence, maple syrup and cacao. Blitz until smooth.

2. Transfer to a glass dish and stir in the dark chocolate chips. Freeze for at least 3 hours. Simply delicious and guilt free.

Healthy apple crumble

SERVES 6

Ingredients

1 cup rolled oats

⅓ cup roughly chopped walnuts

2 teaspoons ground cinnamon

⅓ cup maple syrup

1½ tablespoons coconut oil

Filling

6 cups diced apples

1 tablespoon psyllium husk

2 teaspoons ground cinnamon

Method

1. Preheat oven to 180°C. In a mixing bowl, combine the oats, walnuts, cinnamon, maple syrup and coconut oil.

2. In another bowl, combine the apples, psyllium husk and cinnamon.

3. Transfer the filling to a baking dish and press it down. Place the crumble mix evenly over the top.

4. Bake for 25–35 minutes, or until the apples are tender and the top is golden and crisp.

THE 10:10 DIET MENU PLAN

The 10:10 Diet menu is a carefully designed weight-loss program. While it may seem to be a simple menu to follow, there has been much thought put into making sure that not only are you getting the correct balance of nutrients for healthy weight loss, but you are also eating regularly and it all tastes delicious.

I am a big believer in breakfast in my programs. I have found over years of clinical experience that those who start their day with food, rather than just coffee, tend to take in fewer calories throughout the day. There is research that shows this can be up to 400 calories less. Plus, you are in a better mood and have good energy to enjoy your day, and by the time you get to lunch, you can enjoy it rather than feel ravenous and overeat.

The 10:10 Diet is about healthy weight loss that will successfully make sure you lose fat rather than fluid and muscle.

There is still the inclusion of fruit, with some legumes. Fruit has the fibre that helps keep you full and will allow the sugar release from the fruit to be slower than otherwise, plus it contains wonderful vitamins and minerals.

Nuts and seeds will always play a role as they are great for weight loss, plus are full of magnesium, Vitamin E, protein, good fats and carbohydrates. The diet has been carefully created to take you to the fine line between actually using ketones for fuel rather than glucose, while still being healthy.

Protein is one of the macronutrients that helps keep us full. This is a very important part of healthy weight loss and why protein has the reputation of being fantastic for weight loss. My guidelines are to have protein with each meal and that snacks contain some form of protein that is usually plant-based, such as nuts.

The recommended serving of vegetables of five serves a day is addressed in the menu. Many of the vegetables have been carefully chosen as they are higher in fibre than carbohydrates and sugar.

For people who are vegans or vegetarians but like some of my recipes that contain meat, you can always do a swap to your choice of protein such as tofu or tempeh.

As you can see, there has been much thought to ensure your 10:10 Diet journey is good for your health as well reducing your waistline.

This time around, I have added in some guilt-free desserts. Where you see these on the menu, you will find I have removed the afternoon snack, because, like everything, we need to keep things balanced to continue getting results.

Along with your 10:10 Diet menu planning, it is no problem to repeat meals for shopping convenience or time management. After all, the key to success is preparation.

Here is a four-week sample of the menu.

The menu will include:

- Week 1   Getting started
- Week 2   Introduction to the 600-calorie days
- Week 3   Accelerated weight loss with double 600-calorie days
- Week 4   Your final week before going on to maintenance

WEEK 1: GETTING STARTED

	Breakfast	Mid-morning	Lunch	Mid-afternoon	Dinner
MONDAY					
	Protein shake with antioxidants *(See page 41)*	Boiled egg	Sarah's salmon poke bowl *(See page 51)*	½ protein bar	Steamed vegetables and pork cutlet *(See page 111)*
TUESDAY					
	Sarah's baked mushroom with egg *(See page 27)*	Orange	Tofu sandwich *(See page 66)*	Berries and yoghurt	Sarah's san choy bau *(See page 82)*
WEDNESDAY					
	Sweet and green protein shake *(See page 40)*	10 almonds 1 brazil nut	Leek and mushroom omelette *(See page 72)*	25 grams of cheese with 4 pickles	Salmon patties *(See page 94)*
THURSDAY					
	Boiled eggs and zucchini *(See page 30)*	Apple	Chicken breast and garden salad *(See page 156)*	15 pistachios	Cauliflower mash served with *100 grams of* steak plus ½ cup steamed broccoli plus ½ cup steamed carrot *(See page 91)*
FRIDAY					
	Protein shake with antioxidants	15 pistachios	Eggplant burger *(See page 67)*	Pear	Sarah's broccoli pizza *(See page 84)*
SATURDAY					
	Breakfast salad *(See page 35)*	½ cup strawberries	Baked salmon and greens *(See page 71)*	Cottage cheese and pumpkin seeds	Chicken skewers and Greek salad *(See page 105)*
SUNDAY					
	Sweet and green protein shake	Boiled egg	Sarah's strawberry and chicken salad with mixed roasted nuts and strawberry dressing	½ apple with 1 dessert-spoon nut butter	Sarah's salmon and pesto zucchini noodles *(See page 97)*

WEEK 2: INTRODUCTION TO THE 600-CALORIE DAYS

	Upon waking	Breakfast	Mid-morning	Lunch	Mid-afternoon	Dinner
MONDAY						
	Lemon water	Smoked salmon and asparagus (See page 45)	Apple	Healthy protein salad with chicken, broccoli and quinoa (See page 61)	Boiled egg	Sarah's cauliflower pizza (See page 87)
TUESDAY						
	Lemon water	Protein shake with antioxidants (See page 41)	10 almonds	Tuna and Greek salad (See page 77)	3 celery sticks with 2 teaspoons nut butter	Roasted pumpkin and goat cheese served with 1 cup leafy greens (See page 190)
WEDNESDAY						
	Lemon water	Yoghurt, seeds and fruit (See page 37)	½ cup strawberries	Smoked salmon and garden salad (See page 69)	25 grams cheese with with 1 small cucumber	Sarah's super healthy lasagne (See page 115)
THURSDAY (600-calorie day)						
	Lemon water	Sweet and green protein shake (152 calories) (See page 40)	SKIP	Naked burger (160 calories) (See page 163)	SKIP	Tuna, greens and chilli (152 calories) (See page 164)
FRIDAY						
	Lemon water	Ricotta pots (See page 43)	8 almonds 2 brazil nuts	Healthy protein salad with chicken, broccoli and quinoa (See page 61)	½ protein bar	Almond and cashew-crusted barramundi (See page 103)
SATURDAY						
	Lemon water	Protein shake with antioxidants	10 almonds	Prawn, broccoli fetta and roasted almond salad (See page 63)	1 tablespoon Greek yoghurt with 10 blueberries and a pinch of cinnamon	Easy chicken roast (See page 106)
SUNDAY						
	Lemon water	Sarah's chilli scrambled eggs with fetta (See page 47)	Orange	Stuffed zucchini boats (See page 68)	SKIP	Winter curry (See page 65) For dessert, 2 tablespoons fruit dip with ½ cup strawberries (See page 219)

WEEK 3: ACCELERATED WEIGHT LOSS WITH DOUBLE 600-CALORIE DAYS

	Upon waking	Breakfast	Mid-morning	Lunch	Mid-afternoon	Dinner
MONDAY (600-calorie day)						
	Lemon water	Breakfast muffin (90 calories) (See page 158)	SKIP	Turkey roll-up (181 calories) (See page 174)	SKIP	Chicken meatballs and green salad (260 calories) (See page 161)
TUESDAY						
	Lemon water	Strawberry mint chia breakfast bowl (See page 33)	Apple	Sarah's broccoli and flaxseed salad with 95-gram tin of tuna (See page 60)	15 pistachios	Easy beef stew (See page 109)
WEDNESDAY						
	Lemon water	Energy-lifting smoothie (See page 186)	SKIP	Chicken breast and garden salad (See page 156)	Boiled egg	Ricotta eggplant (See page 90)
THURSDAY (600-calorie day)						
	Lemon water	Sweet and green protein shake (152 calories) (See page 40)	SKIP	Garlic prawn salad (193 calories) (See page 167)	SKIP	Tofu stir-fry (216 calories) (See page 169)
FRIDAY						
	Lemon water	Baked egg (See page 36)	10 almonds	Sarah's strawberry and bocconcini salad (See page 59)	½ apple and 2 teaspoons nut butter	Chicken cacciatore (See page 107)
SATURDAY						
	Lemon water	Protein shake with antioxidants (See page 41)	1 kiwi fruit	Sarah's immune-boosting bowl (See page 54)	7 almonds	Prawn, avocado and lettuce cups (See page 93)
SUNDAY						
	Lemon water	Poached egg and spring onions	½ protein bar	Baked salmon and greens (See page 71)	SKIP	Lamb backstrap and vegetables (See page 117) For dessert, Sarah's cottage cheese mousse (See page 220)

WEEK 4: YOUR FINAL WEEK BEFORE GOING ON TO MAINTENANCE

	Upon waking	Breakfast	Mid-morning	Lunch	Mid-afternoon	Dinner
MONDAY (600-calorie day)						
	Lemon water	1 boiled egg (75 calories)	SKIP	Greek-style omelette wrap (198 calories) (See page 173)	SKIP	One-tray fish and capsicum (290 calories) (See page 175)
TUESDAY						
	Lemon water	Cottage cheese, apple and cinnamon (See page 29)	Vegetable sticks with cottage cheese and turmeric	Sarah's salmon frittata (See page 51)	10 almonds	Chicken, strawberry and avocado salad (See page 101)
WEDNESDAY						
	Lemon water	Boiled egg and zucchini (See page 30)	½ cup strawberries	Cauliflower soup with 100 grams shredded chicken (See page 125)	25 grams cheese with 4 pickles	Sarah's broccoli pizza with a garden salad (See page 84)
THURSDAY (600-calorie day)						
	Lemon water	Capsicum and eggs (200 calories) (See page 178)	SKIP	Spicy silken tofu (214 calories) (See page 179)	SKIP	Oven-baked chilli barramundi (186 calories) (See page 171)
FRIDAY						
	Lemon water	Protein shake with antioxidants (See page 41)	Orange	Tofu sandwich (See page 66)	½ protein bar	Bean and spinach stew (See page 88)
SATURDAY						
	Lemon water	Smoked salmon and asparagus (See page 45)	½ protein bar	Sarah's salmon poke bowl (See page 53)	SKIP	Lamb and broccoli (See page 118) For dessert, Sarah's chia tiramisu (See page 216)
SUNDAY						
	Lemon water	Stress-less smoothie (See page 186)	SKIP	Smoked salmon and garden salad (See page 69)	7 almonds 5 strawberries	Sarah's super creamy green weight-loss soup with 100 grams of protein of your choice (See page 122)

MAINTENANCE

Losing weight when following a plan with compliance will always mean success. There is an end goal in sight, and it is satisfying to achieve your goals along the way. By the end, you have got through a plateau; navigated nights out, restaurants, social gatherings and family dinners; and still got to your goal weight.

But the key now is to keep to your goal weight. Research shows that people who keep to their goal weight for two years will rarely put the weight back on. Other research shows people who also continue their exercise program almost never regain the weight they have lost.

People do have a fear of weight regain as it is so common and not many programs include realistic maintenance.

I have created a formula that is simple and easy to follow to make sure you don't regain the weight.

I still include 600-calorie days in maintenance and believe these should be done twice a week when easing back to eating more complex carbohydrates again and then dropping to once a week in the long term. They are always a great way to keep you on track and include lots of health benefits, such as lowering inflammation, lowering blood pressure, keeping weight stable, healthy aging and increasing neural connections, to name a few.

While maintaining your goal weight I recommend you consume every day:

- 3 servings of protein
- 2 pieces of fruit
- 5–7 servings of vegetables
- 1–2 servings of complex carbohydrates
- 2 servings of good fat (olive oil, nuts)
- 1 serving of dairy.

Following are two sample weeks for maintenance. You can repeat Week 1 for a month if you like and then move to Week 2 for a month.

You will notice I never put a complex carbohydrate in at night. I have never believed we need that food group at night, but I do have a strong belief that we need complex carbohydrates throughout the day as they are the macronutrient that provides us with our much-needed energy.

WEEK 1: MAINTENANCE

	Breakfast	Mid-morning	Lunch	Mid-afternoon	Dinner
MONDAY (600-calorie day)					
	Boiled egg (75 calories)	SKIP	Turkey roll-up (181 calories) *(See page 174)*	SKIP	Chicken pho (298 calories) *(See page 159)*
TUESDAY					
	½ cup cooked oats in water with 1 tablespoon berries	Apple	Sarah's red cabbage, spinach and beetroot salad *(See page 57)*	Kale chips *(See page 207)*	Sarah's san choy bau *(See page 87)*
WEDNESDAY					
	Sarah's wellness smoothie *(See page 185)*	10 almonds 2 brazil nuts	Sarah's salmon poke bowl with ½ cup brown rice *(See page 53)*	Orange	Salmon patties *(See page 94)*
THURSDAY (600-calorie day)					
	Protein shake with antioxidants (120 calories) *(See page 41)*	SKIP	Simple egg salad (200 calories) *(See page 160)*	SKIP	Smoked salmon and greens (205 calories) *(See page 157)*
FRIDAY					
	Strawberry mint chia breakfast bowl *(See page 33)*	Pear and ricotta	Chicken breast and garden salad, rolled up in a wrap *(See page 156)*	10 almonds	Sarah's broccoli pizza *(See page 84)*
SATURDAY					
	Gut-friendly smoothie *(See page 186)*	SKIP	Winter curry with ½ cup rice *(See page 65)*	Cucumber and hummus	Chicken and pear salad *(See page 100)*
SUNDAY					
	2 soft-boiled eggs with a slice of toasted sourdough	Sarah's immunity-boosting slice *(See page 212)*	Sarah's strawberry and bocconcini salad *(See page 59)*	25 grams cheese and pickles	Chicken skewers and Greek salad *(See page 105)*

WEEK 2: MAINTENANCE

	Breakfast	Mid-morning	Lunch	Mid-afternoon	Dinner
MONDAY (600-CALORIE DAY)	Sweet and green protein shake (152 calories) *(See page 40)*	SKIP	Capsicum and eggs (200 calories) *(See page178)*	SKIP	Garlic prawn salad (193 calories) *(See page 167)*
TUESDAY	Baked apple *(See page 42)*	Sarah's immunity-boosting slice *(See page 212)*	Leek and mushroom omelette *(See page 72)*	15 pistachios	Sarah's super healthy lasagne *(See page 115)*
WEDNESDAY	½ cup cooked oats with cinnamon and yoghurt	Banana	Sarah's super healthy lasagne leftovers	½ cup berries with 10 cashews	Fish curry *(See page 99)*
THURSDAY	Cottage cheese, apple and cinnamon *(See page 29)*	Orange	Fish curry leftovers with ½ cup cooked rice	Protein balls *(See page 208)*	Steamed vegetables and pork cutlet *(See page 111)*
FRIDAY	1 slice of sourdough with avocado and tomato	1 Sarah's matcha bars *(See page 209)*	Tofu sandwich *(See page 66)*	Apple	Easy chicken roast *(See page 106)*
SATURDAY	Breakfast salad in a wrap *(See page 35)*	½ cup strawberries	Healthy protein salad with chicken, broccoli and quinoa *(See page 61)*	Banana	Roasted pumpkin and goat cheese *(See page 190)*
SUNDAY	Stress-less smoothie *(See page 186)*	SKIP	Sarah's immune-boosting bowl with ½ cup cooked sweet potato *(See page 54)*	½ protein bar	120 grams steak with 1½ cups steamed mixed vegetables (zucchini, broccoli, cauliflower)

DETOX

I have always loved the concept of a detox for many reasons. One of the main reasons is that I want people to stop and reflect. This reflection is so you will stay focused, keep going on your journey and continue to be your best self. I see detoxing as a holistic approach to health and wellness.

The 10:10 Diet detox guidelines are avoiding alcohol, dairy and gluten, and eating white proteins, lots of greens and foods loaded with antioxidants. For coffee drinkers who can't go without their morning coffee, limit it to just one a day for the detoxing period.

This is a time for you to also detox your home, cosmetics, toxic friendships and cleaning products. Exercise daily is essential, even if it's just a big walk.

Set some goals for yourself and make sure you include doing something you love, such as going to a gallery, movie or museum – whatever brings you laughter and enjoyment.

Apple cider vinegar (ACV) may lower cholesterol, aid weight loss and lower blood sugar, so it is a great addition to enjoy between meals. Plus, studies show it can help keep you full.

If you are not keen on apple cider vinegar, then enjoy some freshly squeezed lemon juice in water, as research shows it can help with weight loss and hydration and is great for your immune system. Alternatively, you can alternate one each mid-morning and mid-afternoon.

DETOX WEEK

	Breakfast	Mid-morning	Lunch	Mid-afternoon	Dinner
MONDAY					
	Detox smoothie *(See page 138)*	ACV drink OR replace with lemon water *(See page 19)*	Detox salad *(See page 140)*	ACV drink OR replace with lemon water	Tofu and bok choy soup *(See page 139)*
TUESDAY					
	Rejuvenating detox smoothie *(See page 138)*	ACV drink OR replace with lemon water	Poached chicken and greens *(See page 147)*	ACV drink OR replace with lemon water	Detox soup *(See page 143)*
WEDNESDAY					
	Detox smoothie	ACV drink OR replace with lemon water	Detox omelette *(See page 152)*	ACV drink OR replace with lemon water	Fish with ginger sauce *(See page 145)*
THURSDAY					
	Rejuvenating detox smoothie	ACV drink OR replace with lemon water	Detox soup	ACV drink OR replace with lemon water	Bean and halloumi stew *(See page 149)*
FRIDAY					
	Detox smoothie	ACV drink OR replace with lemon water	Goat cheese and beetroot salad *(See page 148)*	ACV drink OR replace with lemon water	Salmon one-tray meal *(See page 151)*
SATURDAY					
	Rejuvenating detox smoothie	ACV drink OR replace with lemon water	Detox salad	ACV drink OR replace with lemon water	Poached chicken and greens *(See page 147)*
SUNDAY					
	Detox smoothie	ACV drink OR replace with lemon water	Roasted zucchini filled with bean salad *(See page 153)*	ACV drink OR replace with lemon water	Fish with ginger sauce

TESTIMONIALS

Mother. Nutritionist. Author. These three words give you some insight into the lady behind this book. Then add passionate, creative, inquisitive, generous, dedicated and you now start to see the Sarah Di Lorenzo I know.

When Sarah told me she was writing this series of books, I was thrilled. Not just for Sarah, but for her family as well. They know more than I do of the sacrifices that have brought them to this point. The hours Sarah has spent in her clinic with clients and updating herself with the latest research. Then I came along as the TV producer who took even more of Sarah's precious time due to the hours she would put in to developing a four-minute segment for my show every week.

But there is one theme that reaches out through all of that – and it's love. Love for her family. Love for her clients. Love for her TV segments. Love that I know you will now get to taste through Sarah's magnificent twists on everyday food.

I hope you can feel the love that's gone into every page of this book. Now share your love with family and friends by following Sarah's incredible recipes to make these wonderful tastes and flavours. Savour every mouthful knowing how much has gone into creating these recipes that you now own, too.

Matthew McGrane
TV Executive Producer

It is now eight months since I started your program. I have lost 20 kilograms and am still going! I feel so good! No more aches and pains. I will never be able to thank you enough. You have changed me forever.

Sally
The Sarah Di Lorenzo Community Facebook member

Pancakes, cheese, burgers, muffins. If you love food then the thought of being restricted is petrifying – but Sarah knows all the sneaky tricks to satisfying cravings. Simple tweaks, fun replacements, smart portions – she'll make sure you don't feel like you are missing out. Counting calories and reading nutrition labels is punishment – just stick with Sarah's suggestions and she'll change the way you eat, feel and look. It is pretty incredible. Even if you are a foodie who dreams about pasta, Sarah's program and recipes will get you to your goal and you won't ever be hungry.

Kendall Bora
Executive Producer, Weekend Today, Channel 9

I have lost 22 kilograms. My blood pressure is down from 255/100 (yes, you have read that right) to 150/70. I didn't need meds, just Sarah Di Lorenzo!

Kathy
The Sarah Di Lorenzo Community Facebook member

My journey with you began last year. I had thought you were only for the rich and famous until I started following you on Facebook and Instagram and looked at your program. My weight-gain journey actually began in August 2018, when I was diagnosed with early-stage breast cancer. This resulted in me having to have a double mastectomy and so began my life without being able to exercise. Things weren't straight forward with an infection resulting in more surgery. Then more waiting until I could get my reconstruction done. In December 2019, I got the go-ahead to exercise again, but it didn't seem to matter how much I did or how little I ate, my weight kept climbing. All the things I had done in the past to keep my weight in check no longer worked. This is when you became my lifesaver and threw me a life raft. I will be forever grateful to you. I have lost nearly 14 kilograms and feel amazing.

Lisa,
The Sarah Di Lorenzo Community Facebook member

INDEX

HEALTH INFORMATION

INDEX

RECIPES

INDEX

INDEX

INDEX

INDEX

INDEX

INDEX

INDEX

ACKNOWLEDGEMENTS

The 10:10 Diet Recipe Book has been about acknowledging people who have all been part of the journey with me, people who without knowing it have made an incredibly positive impact on me. All of whom I completely adore.

My beautiful friend inside and out, Monique Wright, who wrote the foreword to my first book, The 10:10 Diet. My inspiration in so many ways, supportive, kind, smart, witty and loyal. Thank you for being on this journey with me.

I want to acknowledge my beautiful friend, Sophie Falkiner, who wrote the foreword to this book. There from the start – kind, thoughtful, supportive, generous, funny and loyal are just a few words to describe Sophie. Thank you .

Sally Bowrey, thank you for again being so incredibly supportive, thoughtful, creative, funny, inspiring, witty and authentic. Thank you for being on this journey with me.

Matt McGrane, I need to acknowledge you for always allowing me to showcase my recipes on Weekend Sunrise, for supporting and believing in me. Thank you, Matt.

Natalie Barr, I want to acknowledge you for, like the other amazing females here, always being such an incredibly supportive friend. Nat is thoughtful, caring and incredibly genuine. Thank you, Nat.

Charmaine Perry, my beautiful friend and producer from my radio days, I want to acknowledge your incredible support from the very start of my media journey and continues today.

And finally Iman Muldoon, another amazing producer who believed and supported me as much as she could from the very start. Thank you, Iman, in my heart and always grateful.

ABOUT THE AUTHOR

Sarah Di Lorenzo is a qualified clinical nutritionist who has dedicated her career to overhauling the health of people of all ages. As well as running a successful clinic in Sydney's Eastern suburbs, Sarah is a regular public speaker and media nutritionist, well known as the resident nutritionist on Channel 7's Weekend Sunrise and a regular on Sunrise. A single mother of three daughters, Sarah is also a regular exerciser and firmly believes in the benefits of a healthy lifestyle.

ALSO BY SARAH DI LORENZO

Available in print, eBook and eAudio
from your favourite bookseller.